Philosophy in 30 Days

Philosophy in 30 Days

DOMINIQUE JANICAUD

Translated from the French by
LISABETH DURING

With a Foreword by
SIMON CRITCHLEY

Granta Books
London

Granta Publications, 2/3 Hanover Yard, Noel Road,
London N1 8BE

First published in Great Britain by Granta Books 2005
First published in France as *Les bonheurs de sophie: une
initiation à la philosophie en 30 mini-leçons*, 2003

1 3 5 7 9 10 8 6 4 2

Typeset by M Rules
Printed and bound in Great Britain by
Bookmarque Limited, Croydon, Surrey

Foreword

The book that you have in your hands is a small marvel. It provides an instructive and delightful introduction to philosophy, divided into thirty short chapters, roughly one for each day of a month. Dominique Janicaud wrote the book in the hope that readers new to philosophy might get a taste for this most enigmatic yet everyday of academic disciplines and be emboldened to explore further.

He wrote it specifically for his daughter, Claire, because she was planning to begin studying philosophy in secondary school – something that is still, sadly, more common in France than in the English-speaking world. Having read the various French philosophy primers and textbooks, he was so dissatisfied with their academic abstruseness that he decided to write his own book, not just for his daughter but for anyone of any age and educational background with some curiosity but little spare time. As the great American philosopher Stanley Cavell put it, 'Philosophy is the education of grown-ups.' The book was written over a month in the summer of 2002 and has, I think, a summery feel, when the exhausting distractions of the daily grind begin to slip away and, in the poet Wallace Steven's words, 'the mind lays by its trouble'. At such moments, one is invited to think: to ponder life's riches and our impoverished understanding of them.

Foreword

Despite its brevity, this book covers a vast range of philosophical authors and topics. The reader will find discussions of ancient and modern philosophy, beginning with the pre-Socratic thinkers, Parmenides and Heraclitus, before moving on to Plato and Aristotle. Janicaud pays particular attention to Plato's use of dialogue, which displays especially well the nature of philosophy as a closely argued dispute about matters of general import, such as beauty, truth and justice. The discussion switches to an elegant survey of modern philosophers, in particular Descartes, Nietzsche, Kant and Hegel. Janicaud then turns to the problems that have occupied thinkers through the ages: the existence of God, the meaning of life, human nature and the question of freedom. We are also given an overview of what takes place under the headings 'Aesthetics', 'Political Philosophy' and 'Philosophy of Science'. Of particular interest is a fascinating discussion of the nature of ethics that offers a lucid engagement with those thinkers deeply suspicious of the whole business of moral prohibition, Freud and Nietzsche.

Yet what I have just said risks skimming the surface of the book and, worse, confirming philosophy in its rather grandiose, inaccessible status. This is what Janicaud calls 'upper-case' philosophy with a capital 'P'. Of more urgent concern is 'lower-case', small 'p', philosophy, which can be shown to be at work in our most everyday activities. What might that mean? Philosophy is not a dogma, a doctrine or a secret wisdom intimated at by gurus; it is not a rite, a ritual or a form of discipleship; nor is it a technique, a method or the private fiefdom of experts on university salaries or working for 'think tanks'. On the contrary, philosophy is an *activity*. It is an activity of thinking, of critical reflection on matters of pressing generality. It is an activity in which all human beings, given the good fortune of the right circumstances, can share. With luck and some persistence, philosophy can become a habit of mind.

For Janicaud, the basic question of philosophy is Hamlet's 'To be or not to be'. That is to say, the many seemingly abstract questions of philosophy circle back and have their roots in the existential question of who we are and what there is. The experience of such questioning can provoke, in Janicaud's words, 'wonder in the face of being, in the face of the very fact that there is being. This astonishment should be hailed and held precious, since it may be the most philosophical act of all.' What is crucial here is that this wonder should be experienced in the face of the *questionability* of things. We do not know for certain who we are and what there is; these are questions for us. The very word 'philosophy' derives from the Greek for 'love of wisdom'. But what is crucial here is that wisdom is not something that we possess or that we know. It is rather something we seek after, of which we are desirous. Philosophy begins in the person of Socrates with an apparent contradiction: the Oracle of Delphi declared Socrates to be the wisest man in Greece, yet he always insistently claimed to know nothing. Yet there is no contradiction between these two positions: wisdom consists in a modesty with regard to what we can know with certainty. This is why Socrates and all the great philosophers refused to think of themselves as sages, which was the role that they attributed to the Sophists, those know-alls who hypnotized people with their flashy charisma. Philosophy is a quest and its itinerary is made up of questions. What is truth? What is justice? What is beauty? What is the right way of organizing society? What can we know of nature? Is there a God? And, finally, who am I? The gloriously presumptuous claim of philosophy is that a life spent rationally thinking through these questions is more fulfilled, richer and happier. For Socrates, the unexamined life is not worth living.

Tragically, the day after the first draft of this book was finished in August 2002, Janicaud died of a heart attack after swimming in the Mediterranean at Éze on the Côte d'Azur. He was sixty-four years old and nearing the end of a highly distinguished academic career at the University of Nice, with a string of highly regarded books to his name. As was his custom, Janicaud had taken a swim after walking what is now called the chemin Nietzsche, the rough, steep path ascending some 1,000 metres from the seashore to the old village where Nietzsche liked to walk during his seven winters in Nice in the 1880s. In the 1980s, I was a student of Janicaud and made this ascent with him on a couple of memorable occasions. Indeed, on a return trip to Nice to take part in a commemoration of Janicaud's life and work, I made the ascent alone. While climbing, I paused to read passages from the book you now have in your hands, which I had just been given by Janicaud's wife, Nicole. I immediately thought that an English translation would be a good idea and I am delighted that this has happened. I very much hope that readers will appreciate being introduced to philosophy in the company of such a good, kind and generous guide as Janicaud.

It is true to say that, like Nietzsche's steep path, philosophy requires effort: it is a labour that requires us to stretch our legs and clear our minds of the fog of our many ordinary entanglements. At its best, and these are the moments one treasures, philosophy can be an ascent. At its beginning in Greece 2,500 years ago, Plato described philosophy as an emergence from the cave of mere illusion and false opinion to the bright light of knowledge and truth. In our more sceptical, lower-case age we might be a little suspicious of the upper-case grandeur of Plato's vision, but we should not deny ourselves the free activity of critical thought that philosophy encourages. Enjoy the climb, but be sure to relax along the way and take in the view of the ground you have already covered.

Simon Critchley
New York City, 2005

Contents

For Claire

1

Philosophy and what it's not

There's a first time for everything: learning to walk, to speak, to say your own name, to recognize your mother and father. But does anyone remember 'first times' such as these? They're too far in the past to seem important, or even to think about now. When you're growing up, other, more memorable events are taking place: your first days at school, your first school play or concert, a family wedding, an emotional crisis, perhaps falling in love for the first time.

Each of these events makes a change, whether big or small, to the pattern of everyday life. When you start to study philosophy, will your day-to-day existence be similarly knocked off course, so that you end up saying, 'Nothing was ever the same afterwards . . .'? It's too soon to tell. But we can see already that unlike the events listed above, the decision to study philosophy has nothing to do with a rite of passage or an initiation ceremony.

A rite of passage is an activity charged with social and religious meaning that must be performed according to established rules. In the Jewish religion, for example, a bar mitzvah marks a young man's acceptance into the community. In certain African societies, practices like infibulation (female circumcision), scarification and tattooing are all irreversible marks of growing up or reaching maturity.

A rite of passage becomes a true initiation ceremony when the group or community uses it to instil in the individual whatever knowledge is necessary to accept him or her as a full member of the group or community. All religions have such rites, as do secret societies and gangs. Look, for example, at Mozart's opera *The Magic Flute*, in which the hero, Tamino, has to submit to a number of symbolic ordeals linked to secret Masonic practices. Once you have gone through these rites, you are 'complete'. You are a different man or woman: an adult, a warrior or an initiate. You know the codes, you've got the passwords.

But becoming a philosopher doesn't involve passwords or a magic formula. There's no tattooing or baptism involved here. There's no need for mass hysteria, for invoking gods or spirits; philosophers don't go in for charismatic trances, ecstatic cries or chantings.

Does this mean that philosophy is too austere for young people, who would rather be having fun? Perhaps. But even when you are young there is more than one side to life. There is room for calm reflection and a touch of seriousness, rather than just action and noise. Discovering that existence can be difficult doesn't have to throw you into a deep depression. Contemplation, critical thought and silence: none of these is necessarily alien to the experience of being young. If you are offered the chance to be more curious, and at the same time more responsible, why not take it?

Philosophy and what it's not

Philosophical reflection is usually associated with clarity of thought and the acceptance of responsibility. It can also certainly inspire passion and enthusiasm, even though it avoids anything that might seem primitive or religious. To become an insider in the world of philosophy, you don't need any special tattoo or sacrament. Philosophy doesn't require militancy and it doesn't depend on the devotion of the masses.

What you can expect to get out of philosophy is only what you put in. In the first place, that means developing a sense of critical detachment, followed by greater intellectual rigour and awareness. These are not things to be sneezed at. Of course philosophy won't promise you everything or permit you anything; but neither should it trouble you or ruin your life. It doesn't operate in terms of 'all or nothing'.

A professor of philosophy is not a high priest who will preach salvation or offer you the moon. Indeed, it's well worth being suspicious of anyone who tries that one on. So, first lesson: beware of gurus.

2

Beware of gurus

In India, a guru is a recognized sage or wise man, a master whom others are willing to follow, sometimes over a long period of time. There are many young people who have embarked on what they considered a 'pilgrimage to the source', as Lanza del Vasto did when, predating the hippies of the 1960s, he tried to escape our noisy and materialistic civilization in search of serenity and the meaning of life.*

This path is worthy of respect. But is it philosophical in the deepest sense of the word? As the search for a kind of wisdom, yes, it is. There are also historical links between ancient Greece and India going back to the time of Alexander the Great's over-reaching and foolhardy expedition in the third century BC. (In fact, the ancient philosophers called Gymnosophists – meaning 'naked wise men' – may have been the disciples or imitators of practices observed in India.)

Often people complain that Western philosophy is too abstract. If this charge is justified, there are good reasons for taking the route of meditation and pilgrimage, and those who find

* Lanzo del Vasto, author of *Le pélerinage aux sources* (Paris, 1947), was the founder of a Gandhian community in France, based on principles of non-violence.

4

their guru and change their life have done something worthwhile.

With that idea in mind, it's a good moment to think about practicalities. If you are going to make such an important decision, it can't be done without a lot of thought. Preparation and care are required to make the move from one cultural tradition to another. For how do you find a genuine guide to life, someone who deserves complete and utter trust?

Such questions are already philosophical, because they lead us to ask about the best route to take to achieve wisdom. They make us aware of what belongs intrinsically to the Western tradition. They encourage us to find out more about the spiritual wealth of India and to think about what we would be looking for in a spiritual master, should we decide to follow that route.

If you are impatient you might understandably protest that, with this method, no one will ever get around to leaving. My answer would be, 'Not necessarily. If you want to go, that's fine. Nothing today is easier or more banal than global tourism. Thousands have done it and will continue to do so. The "results", as we see from experience, are extraordinarily variable, good for some, bad for others, and sometimes tragic. To believe that wisdom will come from simply going somewhere else is an illusion.'

If a critical mind is led only to doubt and scepticism, then it will indeed become a liability. But it is also and overwhelmingly a form of strength if it helps to unmask received ideas and charlatanism.

If it is true that sages and holy men deserve our serious attention, then no one should hesitate to ask questions that might at first seem incongruous: 'What are the criteria upon which I am basing my judgements?' 'What exactly is the line of reasoning I'm following?' 'What if the guru is deluding himself and me?'

In philosophy as in science, whether or not a given explanation is valid doesn't depend on the person who presents it. It's not a matter of age, or tone of voice, or reputation.

If a theorem isn't true just because the maths teacher who expounds it is handsome, then the same goes for philosophy. Does a hypothesis stand up to analysis? Is a line of reasoning absurd? Is a certain thought worth concentrating on? Such questions deserve to be considered for their own sake, freely and calmly. So much the better if the professor is appealing, intelligent and seductive. But don't get the two things mixed up. If someone is presented as a guru, beware!

Everyone knows the famous photo of Einstein sticking out his tongue. He was a great man who could have set himself up as a guru, but he refused to do so. That refusal is a genuinely philosophical attitude. Before Socrates, a philosopher called Heraclitus, known as 'the Obscure', began one of his maxims with these words: 'Not because of me, but because of the Logos.' What he meant was: 'Don't pay attention to me, meditate on what I point towards – the Logos' (for the moment, the least awful translation of this term might be 'the unity of meaning').

So, a critical mind is absolutely essential to a philosophical approach. Thanks to it, any trust you place in this or that professor, this or that master, will be well founded, solid and enlightened. It is this critical mind I want to help you to acquire.

3

Nothing if not critical

Today critical thinking is taken to be an essential element in the economic, political and social life of modern, advanced democracies. Without a critical mind, how can people make reasonable choices for themselves or for others? How can the advantages and disadvantages of a hypothesis or proposition be judged? How can we select our purchases, balance our budgets? From economics to art, from psychology to moral life, if you can demonstrate a critical mind, you know how to get around in the world.

Who would disagree? Well, tyrants and dictators in totalitarian regimes or police states for a start. There's no room for the freethinker in such societies. You have to watch your step, follow the instructions of the big boss or the ruling party.

Yet the contrast may not be that simple. Is it true that a critical mind is the cure-all for every difficulty? We mustn't forget one precondition: the critical mind can't exist without adequate education and training. If you don't know how to read and write, if you have no access to sources of information, how would you demonstrate your powers of judgement if someone just dropped you on the outskirts of a big city? For the destitute, struggling simply to stay alive, the critical mind is more or less meaningless. It's a luxury allowed only in better times, when it's possible to enjoy intellectual and cultural autonomy.

With this in mind, we can see why the spirit of criticism has been completely absent in the great majority of ancient and traditional societies, where authority is wielded by a ruler, a patriarch or a priest. In such tribal or closely linked societies everyone performs their role as dictated by need or ritual. As far as thinking is concerned, only that of the group (or the gods) counts. At the very most, there may be deliberations among the elders, considerations of the most weighty questions. But any idea of a 'critical sensibility', of 'critical thinking', would not only seem incongruous but also be meaningless in such a culture.

This mustn't be allowed to give us a superiority complex, as if we were intrinsically better than other peoples and civilizations. Rather, it should spur us on to greater understanding of the features specific to our civilization.

Once more, we must return to ancient Greece. *Krisis* is a Greek word that means distinction, separation, choice. Of course, not all Greeks showed signs of a critical mind. Yet it was in Athens, at the end of the fifth century BC, that Socrates appeared: a wise man of a new type who never stopped asking questions. His habit of contradicting was disconcerting, as was his way of declaring that he knew that he knew nothing. For his pains, Socrates met with fierce resistance, and he was finally charged and condemned to death for having 'corrupted the young'. But his example survived and his style of discussing things established a following. The 'Socratic dialogue' became a method, even a discipline. Thus the critical mind and the philosophical mind came together in the person of Socrates, a sage who – like Nietzsche – actually wrote nothing himself.

In fact, many years had to pass and many obstacles had to be overcome before the value of the critical mind was admitted. Socrates was way ahead of his time. At the dawn of the modern age, Galileo, who stood up to his judges in asserting that the earth moved around the sun, was only wrong in one respect: being right to contradict established authority.

And it's true even today that an overly critical attitude can be seen as dangerous. Someone who criticizes solely to be negative, to disconcert or to be destructive, will be looked on as a 'nihilist', believing in nothing and destructive just for the sake of it.

How can we find the right way to use our critical mind, which should be considered and used as a valuable attribute? By not turning a means into an end. The critical mind is an instrument. But can it be an end in itself?

Common sense tells us that to criticize only for the sake of criticizing leads nowhere. If this is true, we must follow philosophy via the critical mind and beyond.

The critical mind, then, is a necessary precondition but not in itself enough for an understanding of philosophy. So, we need a bit more philosophy to see further into its meaning as well as its content.

4

A portmanteau word

Some words have a clear and immediate meaning. Thus 'cherry' and 'motorbike' refer, respectively, to a fruit and a means of transport. Even in the more abstract areas, when we read the words 'English' or 'Physics' on a timetable, we know immediately that we are going to learn the English language or to study some of the laws and properties of the material world.

Before going to a philosophy class, do we know what we are going to do and what we are going to study? Not really. The situation is unique and odd. No other discipline is so mysterious.

Why is this? Can the word itself help us here at all?

To begin with, it's a bit disconcerting. The word 'philosophy' is used in a variety of ways, some of which are right and some wrong. It can lend a certain glamour to all sorts of situations. Turn on the radio and you can hear the prime minister putting forward his 'philosophy' of government. On television you will see a government spokesperson saying that the proposed rise in taxes must be accepted 'philosophically'. In the first instance, philosophy is taken to mean 'a general concept': it's vague, but it's a positive 'good thing'. In the second, it has taken on overtones of stoicism of 'being sensible'. Why bring in philosophy if all we want to do is deal in clichés?

Using the word sloppily like this doesn't get us very far. In fact it leads to a kind of wasteland of banality. If this is philosophy, you might as well stay at home and gossip on the phone.

Obviously, philosophy can't be reduced like this. We need to look more deeply into the meanings of this complex and rich word. So, if it's a 'portmanteau word', let's open up the bag . . .

Two things jump out immediately: first, this is a word we have inherited from ancient Greece, and, second, its origin is unambiguously instructive.

The fact that it derives from Greece in the fifth century BC is not insignificant. This is the same region and the same era that gave us Euclidean geometry and the idea of democracy. Philosophy was born side by side with a science that was rigorous and independent, at a time when the attachment to myth was weakening, and people were beginning to demand the banishment of tyranny from political life. This is far from irrelevant. Even today, the triple alliance of philosophy, science and democracy is always fragile and has never been extended over the whole planet. There are still too many dictatorships, too much superstition and fanaticism.

As to the origins of the word 'philosophy', there's nothing mysterious about it: literally, 'philosophy' means the love of knowing or of wisdom. In English we have words similarly ending in *philia*, like the disturbing 'zoophilia' (love of animals) and 'paedophilia' (love of children). This is not love in the best sense of the word. But when love turns towards *sophia*, it loses its sordid side, it reaches for a higher ideal, it seeks to realize a beautiful and good life. How can we translate *sophia* to convey accurately what the Greeks meant?

In our time, wisdom is clearly out of date; it has become – wrongly – the symbol of excessive moderation and balance. For us knowledge itself usually remains something abstract, compartmentalized, for specialists. Have we lost *sophia*'s sense of 'a beautiful equilibrium'?

A fine and noble art of living: that's what the sages of Greece and the earliest philosophers were looking for. Is it too late for us to enrol in their school?

5

Philosophy with a capital 'P'?

Stand in front of a historic building like St Peter's in Rome or the Pyramids, and it's hard not to feel intimidated. Isn't this also the case when we approach the monolith that is Philosophy? Yet, although you can't discover it all at once or in a single place, you can track it down in books. It is linked to the great names: Descartes, Kant and Nietzsche, for example. It comes across as an imposing entity comprising major and difficult texts. How can we approach it? Will we ever be able to get all the way round it?

Historical monuments can benefit from being seen as part of a guided tour. It is convenient, if rather conventional. For most tourists that's good enough. Some would prefer greater freedom, though they might get a bit lost without a guide. With the great philosophical texts – such as the works of Parmenides, Plato or Aristotle – the encounter can be a shock. We run the risk of disorientation. It's normal to look for some help. But 'guided visits' can reduce everything to a few summaries, to brief extracts that make the great authors lose all their vitality and their interest.

Approaching Philosophy can seem to be a much more complicated task than visiting a monument. In both cases, we speak of 'getting an idea of it'. That's easy to say, but can we 'get an idea' of Philosophy as one impressive, unified whole, the essential reference point of our Western culture? As a *tradition*, you might want to say. Perhaps this is even *the* tradition responsible for our ideas and values . . .

Such large words are frightening; they risk paralysing us. We feel the way someone who isn't a rock climber must when faced with a huge wall to be scaled. One way of resolving the difficulty would be to bypass the obstacle. Let's imagine the difficulty resolved. We can let the historical monuments sleep in peace in all their glory.

Rather than putting a capital letter on the word 'philosophy', let's simply decide that it refers to something we can *do*. After all, there are such people: students and professors, of course, but also non-specialists who do it for the love of it. Are they all bookworms, forever running around with huge tomes? Do they have to start quoting Plato or Aristotle, like Molière's ludicrous Master of Philosophy, as soon as they encounter an idea or get into an argument? Can't you be a philosopher just by being clear and using common sense, by being reflective but free of all pretentiousness and jargon?

In the first instance, it's easy to answer yes. But we need to try it out. Philosophize from the ground up? Philosophize without a net? It's only by diving right in, by really trying it out, that one can assess the possibilities and the risks of the enterprise . . .

For the moment, let's write philosophy with a small 'p'. We will leave Plato and Aristotle in the closet. Let's just make do with what's on hand.

6

Trying it out ...

I don't spend much time in the philosophy cafés. But the other day Claire and I were sitting in an unpretentious café in the old town in Nice, after visiting the new Louis Nucéra Library and showing the Museum of Modern and Contemporary Art to Bernie and Judith, our American friends. We'd just seen one of Andy Warhol's most famous 'multiples', the one that reproduces the most stereotypical image of a Hollywood 'star'. As a result, the conversation turned to Marilyn Monroe.

'She was awful!' Claire insisted.

I replied that I disagreed, that I thought she was superb and that even recently she had been voted the greatest beauty of the twentieth century.

'That proves nothing!' Claire retorted.

From then on the conversation got more involved and heated. Bernie maintained that it was precisely her great beauty that made her impossible to represent properly – and it was this aspect that Warhol wanted to communicate with his parodic repetitions.

Judith, on the other hand, found her neither beautiful nor ugly. 'She's the typical American whore, common and vulgar. Since I'm an American woman, I have a right to say so. As for beauty, I don't know what it is, but I won't find out by looking at that Warhol crap. You seem to think you know better. Well, good for you!'

It was a challenge. I wanted to respond by convincing Judith that, at the very least, she couldn't deny Marilyn's physical beauty.

'Yes, but it is such a conventional beauty that she isn't truly beautiful,' she replied. 'Besides, beauty has lost its meaning in the twentieth century . . .'

'It already had in the nineteenth,' Bernie added.

'She is ugly and that's all there is to it,' Claire repeated.

I objected that talking about ugliness implies a certain ideal of beauty, in which case I wanted to know what Claire's criteria were.

To which she replied that there are no criteria for beauty, that everyone has their own ideal.

'But if there are as many ideals of beauty as there are individuals, there's no longer any ideal.'

'If an ideal exists, isn't that just an abstract idea?'

'No, because classical Greek beauty was very close to the ideal, and it wasn't abstract . . .'

'But no one is moved by classical Greek beauty these days. When we talk about beauty to die for, we're thinking of the beauty of youth.'

'We're back to the same old subject – beauty, what's beautiful, what isn't beautiful,' Judith said. 'But after listening to you, I still don't know what beauty is.'

'Look!' said Bernie. 'I just saw one go by. And a redhead what's more. That's unusual.'

Too late! The redhead had already disappeared. We never found out if she would have unwittingly settled our argument. We laughed and admitted that we hadn't made much progress.

'No conclusion, that's always the case with philosophy,' Bernie said.

'But we haven't been doing philosophy,' Claire replied.

'We have, but without knowing it. What is beautiful? What is beauty? I can't help thinking that these are philosophical questions,' I added, while promising to come up with some reasons later, at home.

Socrates and Hippias will help us out.

7

Socrates and Hippias intervene

The scene is Athens. Socrates meets Hippias, who is on his way back from Elis, a city near Olympia, which has chosen him to be its adviser.

Socrates is short, lively, notoriously ugly. It's obvious he takes no interest in his appearance. Hippias, haughty and conceited, thinks of himself as somebody important. As a famous Sophist, he believes in the unsurpassed brilliance of his courtroom oratory; he is blissfully confident that he can work his way out of any problem, however thorny. (Today he would be an international lawyer or a consultant for one of the multinationals.)

Next to this braggart, Socrates feigns modesty and pretends to be confused. He confesses that he doesn't know how to answer the question 'What is beauty?'

For Hippias, nothing could be easier. Characteristically, he responds as if the question were 'What is beautiful?' Answer: a beautiful young woman.

Hippias doesn't notice the difference between the two questions. He responds with an example of beauty when the question is about beauty itself. Socrates quickly provides some further examples. Can a pot be beautiful? Can the beauty of a young girl be compared to that of a goddess? If we don't concentrate on the question of what makes a beautiful thing beautiful, we will simply slip from example to example without ever finding a firm criterion.

Hippias thought the question concerning beauty was easy, but in fact he's getting nowhere. Socrates presses him for a better definition. Hippias reckons he has come up with something: it's gold that makes things beautiful! To this Socrates objects that Phidias' statue of Athena, which is universally admired, is not gold but ivory.

Hippias, now forced on to the defensive, tries a more abstract definition: appropriateness. Yet this is hardly an improvement. Isn't a wooden ladle in fact more appropriate than a golden ladle? At this, Hippias takes refuge in values he considers indisputable. For him wealth and honours come first; lower down the list are utility and advantage.

Socrates has no trouble coming up with further examples to show that none of these qualities applies universally. It's the same story up to and including the last definition considered: that beauty is what delights the ear and the eye. At the end of the dialogue we are led only to an acceptance of failure. Socrates knows that there is no answer.

Is Hippias right? By multiplying his objections, has Socrates shown that he's unable to understand the bigger picture, the overall unity of the subject? At the very least, Socrates has succeeded in one respect: he has made us aware of the difficulty of proceeding from the observation of beautiful things to an understanding of the essence of beauty itself.

This question has been debated for 2,500 years. Just because it has never been satisfactorily resolved, does that mean we shouldn't raise it again? And the other day, coming out of the Museum of Modern and Contemporary Art, did we make any progress?

8

Difficult or simple?

Is Plato a difficult philosopher? Although he has written complex and subtle dialogues, the one we have just been discussing, the *Hippias Major*, is not among the most daunting. When we marvel at beauty, we transcend mere differences of taste and are led to wonder whether there is in the beautiful an intrinsic coherence and harmony. It does not take great subtlety to understand this.

When I was an adolescent, I tried to begin with Plato's philosophy. But I made the mistake of reading an academic introduction rather than the text itself. I recall my amazement at 'the theory of ideas'. The exposition I had read was so unconvincing that I could not understand why the ideas existed on their own, forming a kind of 'heaven'. We have many ideas, I said to myself, they come and go, some are valid and others not; why should we imagine that they can become universal models, that they might even be divine?

What I didn't understand at first was that a Socratic dialogue does not usually lead to a definitive conclusion. It does something else: through its irony, it clarifies our thinking. At its best, as Plato sees it, it is only a preparatory stage for the theory of ideas. In the *Hippias Major*, as in many other Socratic dialogues, the theory of ideas does not even make an appearance.

It is also important to understand that Plato does not elevate every kind of 'idea' to the ultimate position. There are certain ideas we need to keep returning to for inspiration. They are unique in having their own intrinsic coherence; they are valid in and of themselves. I can observe and draw any number of round shapes and circles, but there is only one idea of a circle.

But does this idea of a circle have an existence somewhere, materially speaking, like the wheel I see in front of me when a car stops outside the café where I am drinking a beer? How do we conceive this idea of a circle that I have, and you have, that we share and have shared from the first moment when we understood what a circle was? How do we conceive it? What status do we give it?

I cannot see with my own eyes the idea of a circle. Nor do I see with my own eyes the incontrovertible truth that $2 + 2 = 4$. Nonetheless, to understand this idea, to grasp this truth, is well and truly to *see* what is coherent about it and the way it contributes to an explanation of reality.

We say 'I see' when we think we have grasped something; and this understanding, to which others will be added, means we are no longer completely lost in the everyday world, which we take to be the real world.

This 'seeing' has to do with intelligence. It is not insignificant, because it opens a host of new possibilities to us. In the absence of calculation or any form of mathematics, if we don't have any idea about the real, we might well be helpless and paralysed, having nothing to go on but our unreliable sensations and arbitrary whims.

Difficult or simple?

Socrates begins to marvel at the new and immense horizons that open up to the mind when it *understands*. For Plato the world of ideas is an unexplored terrain that holds the key to everything.

Why is it hard for us to imagine the intensity of this wonder? Because the world of ideas and concepts has become too familiar to us. Knowledge and the sciences have developed to the point that we are now blasé about all things intellectual, as if we could simply be indifferent to all of humanity's achievments.

Most of us have a utilitarian view of ideas. (They help us to understand things, to control things, to make plans, to devise techniques and technical instruments, etc.) But Plato has a vision of ideas that is enthusiastic in the literal sense of the word: they are possessed by a god. If he doesn't quite worship them, he still believes they possess a divine power, and he never fails to admire them in their unity and harmony.

Of course, we have trouble imagining such a state of mind. (Remember that for Plato the stars themselves were divine beings.) How can we put ourselves back into the way of thinking that such a belief implies without upsetting our normal mindset? It is going to take a strenuous effort to leave behind our familiar intellectual terrain.

But if we do, we may find that philosophy is for the mind what a trip to exotic places is for the body. Coming home from a holiday in the Caribbean, haven't you gained something: relaxation, a tan, distraction? With philosophy, the benefit is, quite simply, understanding.

Difficult or simple?

It is said that a true idea is luminous. If so, then anyone can experience it just by using their intelligence a bit.

A ray of Platonic light is not yet complete illumination. There is still a long way to go. After all, at the end of the *Hippias Major* Socrates warns us, 'All that is beautiful is difficult!'

9

The gallery of great minds I:
some philosophical stars
of antiquity

Perhaps now is the time to get to know some of the great
philosophers, our guides on the road to knowledge and wisdom.

Hegel said that the history of philosophy is like a gallery of
the great minds who have ennobled humanity. Let's hope he was
right. We will assume that the first thing required is to acknowledge these great men with gratitude and admiration.

I prefer not to introduce them solemnly but just as I see them,
indeed as the seventeenth-century philosopher Blaise Pascal saw
them: charming and well-mannered men whom we'd like to know
and listen to, more like older brothers than severe teachers.

We have already met Socrates and the Sophist Hippias
(who was not a great thinker). We must go back even further in
time, to the sixth century BC, to find two other major figures of
Greek philosophy: Heraclitus and Parmenides. Who was actually the founder of philosophy? For a long time this question
would have received the reply, 'Plato'. Now we are more aware
of the importance of earlier thinkers. Even Socrates himself was
not the first sage in Greece.

However, Socrates was the first to engage with the crowd, the first to practise the dialogue of contradictions known as the dialectic. Before Socrates, the sage was not such an approachable figure.

Heraclitus, famous for his obscure, pithy thoughts, was rumoured to be proud and contemptuous of the public, but he must have had a taste for mischief. One anecdote tells us that while he was warming himself at his modest fireplace, some travellers – who had come out of their way to see him – hesitated in the doorway. He invited them to come in, saying, 'There are gods here too!'

The most daunting sage was probably Parmenides, whom Plato looked on as a father (even if that required his symbolic 'murder'). Parmenides founded a philosophy school at Elea in Graeca Magna, south of Naples. Perhaps I should say that it was there he founded philosophy itself when he uttered the statement, 'Being is and non-being is not' – a proposition at one and the same time hopelessly abstract and absolutely obvious.

His dense *Poem* is all the more enigmatic since we have only fragments of it. It is like a magnificent temple destroyed by the passage of time and the ravages of history.

Perhaps now is the moment to reintroduce Plato. He has already appeared, of course. But it's typical that he made his appearance in a dialogue in which Socrates is the protagonist and where he never speaks in his own voice Even his most difficult and complex dialogues, like *The Republic* (not to speak of *The Sophist* or *Parmenides*) do not – strictly speaking – present his own doctrines. Platonism certainly existed as a doctrine, because the

Academy, the school founded by Plato, survived until the very end of the ancient world and enjoyed an extraordinary influence, as it still does today. But Plato's method is the dialogue. And the author is hidden behind his characters, often disguised by his ironic tone.

Who was Plato himself? How should we imagine him? He was a vigorous man who stood up to a tyrant, Dionysius of Syracuse, whose city he wanted to reform. He was sold into slavery and then bought back. I see him as the most aristocratic of philosophers, a man of great nobility, far-sighted and deep, with a keen sense of irony.

Aristotle, his student, also had an exceptional destiny (since he was the tutor of the future Alexander the Great and was, for many centuries, considered *the* philosopher). He was a brilliant and subtle teacher. A comment has been ascribed to him: 'Plato was my friend, but my greatest friend was the truth.' I see him as discreet and calm, impressive wholly through the power of his thinking, fascinating his pupils with his precise and encyclopedic mind. He was a logician, a physicist, a biologist and a political theorist. He reconstructed both ethics and 'first philosophy' (which was not yet called metaphysics). No subject of inquiry was foreign to him. It is not surprising that he has had such an impact on posterity.

Yet the ostensible 'continuity' of the tradition is not something we should have any illusions about. Since the death of Aristotle, there have been many interruptions, countless things forgotten, and innumerable political and human dramas: Greece lost its political independence, the Roman Empire itself collapsed, the library of Alexandria was destroyed by fire, Europe fell before the great invasions, and much else.

The advent of Christianity as the dominant and then the exclusive religious doctrine must have shattered the bonds connecting cultivated Romans with their Greek philosophical sources, sources whose extraordinary richness has only been sketched here in the most schematic fashion. The Church Fathers attempted, in weaving these threads anew, to turn them to their own advantage. But it was much later, and then thanks only to Arab sources, that Aristotle was translated into Latin. The roundabout routes that history has imposed! There have been so many obstacles between us and knowledge of Greek philosophy and its central texts.

10

The gallery of great minds II: some modern stars

Now, making a huge leap in time, we come to some of the important modern philosophers. The interval between the third century BC and the seventeenth century of our era is easy to calculate: 2,000 years. But this doesn't mean that no work of value was produced between the death of Aristotle and the birth of Descartes.

Such an idea would be neither plausible nor reasonable. Significant philosophical schools appeared and evolved in Greece and in the Roman world: Stoicism, Epicureanism and Neoplatonism. The lengthy period known as the Middle Ages (for want of a better name) had its own moments of intense intellectual activity. From Damascus to Andalusia, from Toledo to Paris, from Oxford to Louvain, there were translations of ancient philosophy and commentaries on them: each of the three monotheistic religions (Judaism, Christianity and Islam) displayed extraordinary theological finesse; algebra was invented and disseminated in the Arab world; the Christian West gradually revived the inspiration of the ancients while making progress in experimental knowledge of the natural world.

So why do so many philosophy textbooks jump almost directly from antiquity to the modern period? Haven't I just done the same thing, oversimplifying a rich and complex history?

My response is simple. It is precisely the complexity of this history that makes it inaccessible and difficult for beginners. Moreover, many secondary school and university students lack the religious background essential for even the most rudimentary sympathy with the profoundly theological ideas of the Middle Ages. For example, St Augustine and St Thomas Aquinas were remarkable thinkers, but they were also men of deep faith, and their work is so permeated by knowledge of the Holy Scriptures and debates within the Church that direct access to their texts is almost impossible.

But with Descartes, a man of the modern age *par excellence*, things are totally different. He is typically modern because he wanted to start again from scratch. He received an exemplary education in the classics from the Jesuits, as he relates in his famous *Discourse on Method* (written in French, which was in itself a revolutionary act in the period). But he found that the vast bulk of the material he was taught (including philosophy) appeared to have shaky foundations.

Descartes wasn't satisfied with what was merely probable; he wanted to know the truth, and to know it clearly and distinctly. Only mathematics, because of 'the certainty and evidence of its reasoning', would do.

From this, only two possibilities were open to Descartes: either he could pursue mathematics alone and abandon everything else; or he could take mathematics as his model and perfect a method in line with the 'right guidance of reasoning' in both the sciences and the conduct of life.

If Descartes had not chosen this second path, he would still be known today as the inventor of analytic geometry, rather than the founder of modern philosophy. He would be surprised to find that his real fame rests on his philosophical work, and that the scientific research he valued most has been relegated to the background.

A century later, moving to the east, to Königsberg in Prussia (now Kaliningrad in Russia), we must pay tribute to another giant of modern philosophy, Immanuel Kant.

Also a man of great learning – simultaneously a mathematician, a physicist, and a geographer – Kant became an original philosopher relatively late in life (his greatest work, the *Critique of Pure Reason*, was published when he was over sixty). Personally, he had nothing of Descartes' manly and military character. Short, physically frail, a bachelor, methodical to the point of obsession (his daily walk was renowned), Kant was every inch the eminent professor.

His great reputation comes from the fact that his critical enterprise was conducted with a logic, a rigour and a precision that have never been matched. Applying the same critical method to practice as to theory, he re-established morality on rational foundations, and rounded off his grand structure of knowledge by examining aesthetic judgement and the meaning of harmonious order in the sphere of natural phenomena. After Kant, nobody would ever do philosophy in the same way.

Every great philosopher shakes up the intellectual landscape and forces his contemporaries to ask questions in a new way. This was also the case with Hegel, the other great German professor, who was thirty years old in 1800. He was formed by the eighteenth century, but in his audacity he was a philosopher of the future (his dialectic was to be a powerful influence on socialist and revolutionary thought).

In his youth, Hegel was already nicknamed 'the Old Man', which doesn't sound very attractive. His originality stemmed from the fact that he didn't allow his personal tastes to dominate, but recorded what he called 'the truth of the Whole'. Reason must learn to be reconciled with even the most contradictory of realities. For Hegel, these realities included logical conditions and physical structures, not to mention the totality of the psychological, moral and political spheres. Perhaps there is something excessive about this vast systematic enterprise. Yet it still fascinates and inspires, even when its central notion of contradiction itself keeps being contradicted.

I should have liked to introduce Nietzsche here as well, but I realize that this chapter has gone on long enough. In any case, it's not possible to pay tribute to Nietzsche in a rush. I promise not to forget about him, though – he will get a whole chapter to himself later.

One last word. Pascal remarked that we moderns are dwarves standing on the shoulders of giants, the ancients. This image provides an overarching justification for our study of the great philosophers. Without them, we would have to reinvent everything. With them, we are already starting off higher up.

Yet we need to know how to read them advisedly, without letting ourselves be overwhelmed by the weight of this tradition.

11

History or analysis?

When we encounter these famous thinkers, there is a risk that we will find ourselves at a loss, capable only of expressing admiration or uttering hollow tributes. We may repeat a few philosophical formulae or striking phrases but without thinking for ourselves and without understanding what philosophy is about.

We must face this problem squarely. It is a question vigorously debated today by professional philosophers. Some, in what is known as the 'continental' tradition (mainly the Germans and the French), believe good, solid philosophy cannot be produced without reference to the history of Western thought. If we go back to Hegel, we remember his claim that philosophy and the history of philosophy, properly understood, are one and the same.

Other philosophers, primarily allied to the Anglo-Saxon tradition, hold that the essence of philosophy is the analysis of concepts and the exchange of arguments.

At first glance, neither of these camps is wrong. We may wonder if the partisans of the history of philosophy could really get by without argument and, on the other hand, if minds that are primarily logical and analytical wouldn't benefit from more than a quick backward glance at the status of the questions they're considering.

Common sense would seem to argue in favour of a compromise between the two 'camps'. And this is the direction in which we are going to go.

Eminent scientists often jump recklessly into the philosophical arena. They think the history of philosophical problems can easily be ignored. The results are sometimes catastrophic. This is because philosophical reflection requires rigour in the use of terminology: essential terms must be all the more precisely defined because of the richness and often ambiguous nature of our 'natural' languages (French, English, German and so on). Take, for instance, the word 'sense': it can refer to meaning or significance (something has a certain 'sense' in a certain context) and also 'sense' in and of itself (taken as a value, as in 'that makes sense'), but it also indicates the realm of perception and the organs that enable us to see, hear, touch and so on.

I can illustrate the necessity of clarification with an anecdote. One day in an American university a professor announced a new course on 'The Meaning of Life'. A number of students rushed to join the class, because there had recently been a suicide on the campus and they thought the professor would finally tackle that most important of all questions: does life have a meaning? Shortly after the course began, the lecture theatre emptied as the students found themselves disappointed: the professor had announced that his course would deal with the grammatical and logical meaning of the *expression* 'the meaning of life'.

History or analysis?

This professor represents analytic philosophy, a form of philosophy so concerned about clarity that it endlessly examines and explains its vocabulary, patiently refining its arguments. It is certainly true that it would be naive for any discourse to believe it can take up the serious questions without preliminary explanation. I've seen myself how such naivety leads straight to catastrophe, or else to emptiness and insignificance.

But should explanation be solely analytic and argumentative? If so, it risks turning the means into an end (reasoning well without knowing what for) – and also risks forgetting the lessons of the history of philosophy.

On the other side of the fence, should philosophy be exclusively historical? Here, repetition or dogmatism is the danger: 'The master said this', 'Descartes said that' and so on. What would become of our critical mind? What would happen to the hard work that goes with reasoning?

There can be no good history without analysis and no philosophical analysis without accepting the need to engage in dialogue with – and confront – the great ideas of the past.

12
Why?

Young children often ask annoying questions. In particular, they like to ask 'Why?' at every turn and about anything at all.

Unprepared parents find themselves obliged to provide answers. 'Why do butterflies have wings?' the little girl asks. 'To fly,' the irritated mother answers. 'Why is the sky blue?' 'Because that is the colour of the oxygen which forms the earth's atmosphere,' answers the father, proud of his scientific knowledge.

We would be satisfied if the child were happy with the answers. But if the questions keep coming – 'Why must animals fly?', 'Why is oxygen blue?' – we are tempted to reply, 'Just because!' to shut them up. It's an answer that amounts to saying, 'No more questions.' The demand for a reason or an explanation is met with the bald, 'That's how it is because that's how it is.'

The child is amazed. He's not satisfied to learn that butterflies simply fly and that the sky just is blue. In this sense, isn't he already a bit of a philosopher in his own way? Didn't Plato remark that the fundamental attitude of the philosopher is wonder? In fact, if you never wonder at anything, you will never ask any questions, you will find everything 'normal'. You will simply register what's there. This is certainly less tiring than trying to understand it.

But to wonder just for its own sake, and at everything and anything, is not the attitude of a lucid and responsible adult. It's probably the easiest way to look like a fool or an airhead. Don't we need to learn how to ask 'good questions', pertinent questions?

But what is a pertinent question? How can we judge? And above all, what differentiates between a common-sense question, a scientific question and a philosophical question?

'Why are you going into the sun?' 'Because I want to get a tan.' We would be stuck at the level of banal experience

'Why do all bodies fall?' 'Because of the law of falling bodies: proportionate to their mass and in inverse proportion to the square of their distance.' Here, with Newton's universal law of gravitation, we have reached the peaks of modern physics.

'Why does the world exist?' (No answer: the question is too philosophical. It doesn't seem soluble.)

Is philosophy unique in being unable to answer its own questions? If they can't be answered, wouldn't it be preferable to stop asking them?

Certainly, the question 'Why?' is awkward. Next to it, the question 'What is this or that?' seems completely sensible: it is content to search for the essential constituents of a thing (its essence). The question 'Why?' is more ambitious, but equally ambiguous: it is asking simultaneously about the cause and the purpose.

The universal law of gravitation allows us to understand how the immense machinery of nature functions in one of its most important aspects. Thanks to its admirable power to describe and explain, it is the perfect answer to the question

'How?': in other words, to the search for a reason in the clearly deterministic world of bodies in motion relative to one another. However, it pushes to one side the question 'Why?' in its second sense: 'What is sought by the application of this law? For what purpose do bodies obey such a law?'

I have deliberately left unanswered questions of this order, which transcend the sphere of experience. Was I right or wrong? If I am behaving scientifically, I am right: science cannot and should not respond to questions concerning the possible projects of God or nature.

Was I wrong, however, to abandon the idea of responding as a philosopher? In actual fact, I acted like a critical philosopher in the Kantian sense, or even in the positivist sense. The ultimate questions dealing with the meaning of the universe, the possible existence of God, the possible survival of the soul, are questions insoluble for us humans within the limits of our finite knowledge. Philosophy, therefore, should not go beyond these limits.

Yet this has not always been the attitude of philosophers, and even today it is not invariably the case. Quite the contrary, the philosophers known as metaphysicians did claim they could provide definitive and confident answers to these questions. At times they have reached remarkable heights of ingenuity. This is true of Leibniz, for example. To the question 'Why is there something rather than nothing?' (another way of positing the question 'Why does the world exist?') he replied, 'Because of the principle of the best of all possible worlds.'

Now, is this principle as arbitrary and ridiculous as a reading of Voltaire's *Candide* would lead us to believe? Poor Candide lives through the most awful events, and his tutor, Pangloss, a discipline of Leibniz, continually justifies all these evils in the name of the famous Leibnizian law. The comedy is very effective. Yet we are more Leibnizian than we think whenever we analyse the meaning of a series of events and find that, to understand it, the sense of the action requires that some suffering be tolerated in order to achieve a higher objective. But Leibniz went much further than that, since he argued that God created the world by following this 'logic of the best', and it becomes for him a key to everything. Thus he could respond with an indisputable answer to the question of the ultimate origin of all things, and why they exist.

I do not deny that following our question so far risks taking us beyond what we can determine and beyond the very limits of our experience. Precisely on that account it responds to an uneasiness that has never ceased to haunt the human race, and that keeps resurfacing (often in much less respectable forms than that of Leibnizian philosophy, in the fascination for the paranormal or as charismatic religion).

Metaphysics is the part of philosophy that contemplates ultimate questions, those that deal with the meaning of life, the existence of God, the immortality of the soul, the unity of the world. For some, it is the crowning achievement of philosophy; for others, it is philosophy's most dangerous and illusory temptation. At the very least, we need to be aware of the problem.

13

What is man?

Continuing with the question 'Why?', especially when the subject is man, we may well keep coming up against the same brick wall. It is an unanswerable question. Or rather, it is a question that only religion or metaphysics can claim to answer.

This time we are going to be more modest and pose only the question 'What is it?' when the subject is us. There are more than enough difficulties to face here.

Who are we? In so far as we make up a species, we are distinguishable from other animals: whatever our skin colour, our size and the other details of our 'particulars', we share physical features with those like us. Our upright stance differentiates us from the apes, even the higher apes. Human offspring are born naked and fragile; they take much longer to become adult than those of other animals.

But is it only physical characteristics that distinguish us from other animals? Are we even animals first and foremost? What makes us human is the use of an articulate language. Even if some higher mammals, certain birds and dolphins have a kind of language, only man invents and develops articulate symbols granting him the possibility of an open-ended, indefinitely perfectible communication.

This is the classical definition of man as the 'speaking animal', and it has a lot to recommend it. However, it is not the only one possible. Man is also a political animal, a laughing animal, a technical and artistic animal, even a mad animal. Laughter is peculiar to man, as is the explicit concern for political life, the capacity to transform the environment via tools and instruments, the creation of beautiful works for the sake of pure enjoyment and even, finally, the madness that attacks only that animal capable of reasoning and of becoming rational.

However, the question concerning the human condition is not exhausted by listing a certain number of qualities – or flaws. Before the invention of a specialized science studying *anthropos* (Greek for man) via his different morals and customs, languages and social and familial structures, the dominant opinion was that there was something called 'human nature', meaning a permanent reservoir of anthropological characteristics to be found from one end of the planet to the other, no matter what the stage of cultural development. If man was created by God, didn't all descendants of Adam possess the same core of humanity, even if their histories had been strikingly different in terms of culture, wealth and development?

More and more discoveries of ancient sites and human remains have proved that the human species is much older than we used to think. Accordingly, our 'age' as a species has increased considerably: we are now possibly 6 or 7 million years old.

This realization, combined with innumerable studies of our prehistory, shows how far becoming human was a matter of perfecting tools. First it was stones, then metal – bronze and iron – and with the use of tools came settled communities, the invention of writing and agriculture, then the state and its political authority, and finally, after 3,000 years, we catch up with history – something we know a lot more about, for better or for worse, than those distant times we call prehistory.

All this information leads us to believe that man today is nothing but the product of a biological evolution that became cultural, technological and symbolic, an evolution that continues. Don't we notice incredible transformations? Aren't we becoming more and more communicative creatures who tomorrow, thanks to prostheses and the new miracles of biotechnology, will find our health, performance and even longevity unimaginably improved? Will this technological progress lead us to a state of 'super-humanity'?

It's tempting to adopt such a view. However, when we come back down to earth and look objectively at the lives of those rapidly diminishing populations whose existence is still very close to that of the Stone Age, we are surprised by the intelligence and maturity of groups who used to be called 'primitive'. Recently, there was a documentary on TV about a remote region of New Guinea where there were certain tribes who had never seen white people and their technologies. Witnessing the encounters between these supposedly primitive people and the 'civilized' people who are extremely proud of their cameras and recording equipment, not to mention their weapons, you have to wonder who is more intelligent. Which group is most vain about its achievements? Which stands out most for its guile? Where do we find more wisdom and good sense? Which group is more naive, brutal, crude? You can guess that the answers don't automatically confirm our idea of 'progress'.

The question 'What is man?' can't be answered by anthropology, or by any of the sciences that help us better to understand the various human types in their environment, their prehistory and their history. But at least these sciences help us to explain how man lived, how he developed and diversified, etc. That is no small achievement.

And what of philosophy? Does it hold the answer? No. But at least it can synthesize all this data and develop an agenda worth pursuing. Yet there is one more thing, something I almost forgot. At times philosophy does believe it has found the key to the humanity of man: freedom.

14

What is freedom of action?

Freedom is a big word, though we see examples of it around us every day. But to what degree are the examples we see manifestations of true freedom?

The first reaction of most young people is to think that freedom means the absence of constraints. To be free is to do what you want, when you want, the way you want: without being monitored by parents, teachers or big brothers. And above all freedom means not having to work.

It's a perfectly understandable attitude, but it doesn't really capture what freedom is. The stakes are pretty high. Does freedom simply mean refusing anything imposed on us by other people? Shouldn't freedom contain something positive in relation to others and to ourselves?

To think oneself free is not necessarily the same as being truly free. Am I free in relation to my instincts, my basic desires? I am influenced by my membership of a group, by images, by opinions expressed on TV and so on. The Dutch philosopher Spinoza showed that the human condition is dependent on its relation to natural conditions and man's own passions. Yet he believed that understanding these dependencies teaches us what it is to be free. A clear-sighted acceptance of the inevitable is the highest form of freedom.

I can choose either to understand or to misunderstand what happens to me. Thus the notion of choice is essential. On the one hand, it implies that I retain the power of decision; on the other, I am never faced with only one single and exclusive possibility. When 'I have no choice', it is because I have realized, correctly, that no viable alternative is open to me.

There is only freedom of choice when the options are not equivalent and the choice will make a difference. Between the plague and cholera, do I simply toss a coin? Since the Middle Ages, the classic example used has been the story of Buridan's ass. Offered either oats or hay, the animal, which was equally fond of both, died because it did not know how to choose. It is true that there are cases where the stakes appear equal on both sides and the only way out of an awkward situation is to ask, 'Heads or tails?' The answer is a matter of chance, but the choice of method is itself an act of freedom.

Perhaps we are beginning to have a better sense of what makes an act free. First of all, it must have been willed, decided upon. A reflex is not free: if fire burns me, I pull my hand away. On the other hand, if, because of some crazy bet, I keep my hand in the fire to prove my courage, this is an act of freedom.

We can now see another condition of free action: motivation. At a crossroads, how can I decide which route to take if I don't know how to read the local alphabet? Or again (something that happens in the USA), if I have no map indicating which route leads where since the signs show only the numbers of the highway? Does acting freely mean acting with knowledge of the facts? If I am supposed to vote, for example, shouldn't I become informed about the candidates and their policies?

When you are young, you start off by thinking you are free when you reject all constraints; later you understand that certain constraints, those you learn to impose on yourself, may allow you to discover new possibilities in life. Why not? This prospect isn't impossible to imagine. The freest act is the most clear-sighted act, the act chosen for its own sake. Why don't we consider the decision to think freely and disinterestedly, the act of philosophizing, as precisely one of the freest of all possible acts? It is an act through which I become fully autonomous – that is, capable of legislating my own actions.

If not all acts are free in the same way, should freedom itself depend on the degree of enlightenment it brings? Or is every man essentially free in so far as he is a man? If this is the case, we must not simply identify the capacity for being free with the enactment of freedom. We still don't know how freedom can be made concrete in the world.

15

Moral freedom, political freedom

When I set even the most basic rule or standard of behaviour for myself (for example, I must stop wasting time in the street chatting with people I bump into), I am exercising my freedom. Is that sufficient?

The rules of practical conduct are only maxims, Kant told us. They are absolutely relative. We must ascend to a higher level, to the level of the moral law itself.

According to Kant, I am not truly autonomous if I am not aware that the very principle of my action depends on my will. My actions will be valuable (in my own eyes) only if they follow the promptings of my conscience.

To say that I am responsible means that I can vouch for my own actions and justify them. When I take responsibility for my freedom, I must constantly question my relations to others. Moral freedom is a freedom vis-à-vis others and for others.

But what makes this freedom moral? The word 'moral' hasn't always had a good press, especially with young people. 'Moralize' means to give advice that is annoying because it is constraining. We are back to constraint.

As a matter of fact, when we talk about moral freedom, the narrower problem of moral conduct and its rules is only part of the picture. The term 'moral' indicates that this freedom is characteristic of individuals engaged in interpersonal relations and who have habits and customs (in Latin *mores*). So moral freedom reflects a general fact about us: that we live in a society made up of free individuals who, as members of society, must accept or reject a certain number of rules and forms of behaviour. Moral freedom is the general framework of any society whether or not it has the power to exercise freedom (in the strict sense).

So how do we get from moral freedom to political freedom? Well, of course, things don't happen just like that. It's not as if first of all you have responsible subjects and then you get society. Clearly, in advanced societies like ours, you can decide to create any number of associations, from athletics organizations to arts organizations. But the phenomenon called 'the body politic' doesn't arise in such an artificial fashion. Before individuals demanded their freedom, there were city-states, kingdoms and then states.

Without going too far back, let's think about antiquity again. In Egypt, for many centuries, the Pharaoh relied on a priestly caste to preserve the dominance of a hierarchical order. In such a society there is no such thing as a free subject. Political freedom in the modern sense was not universal even in Greece. It certainly did not exist in Sparta. Even in Athens, where democracy was founded, the institution itself appears only in the fifth century BC, after which it was constantly threatened and subjected to challenge. Major political thinkers, Plato and Aristotle were not democrats: they favoured rule by an elite, be it authoritarian or moderate. By the time we get to Rome, even under the Republic only the citizen is considered free. But he has duties towards the city and the exercise of his freedom depends strictly on those duties, on his responsibilities and office, and on his place in the city.

From a political point of view, freedom is not only a very late acquisition (not until the eighteenth century could it become a principle, with the American and then the French revolutions) but also painstakingly defined and circumscribed. Each individual is free only as long as his freedom doesn't endanger the freedom of others. And 'freedoms' can be defined as guarantees offered by a civilized state to every subject or citizen as long as everyone respects the common rules. To take just one example, the *lettres de cachet*, which allowed the king to throw anyone he pleased into prison without giving a reason, were abolished by the French Revolution. The freedom that replaced it, the *sûreté*, means that I can no longer be arrested without due process being observed. Sadly, the French Revolution itself was not good at setting an example . . .

Political freedom can exist only in a stable state where, by law, each member is promised well-defined rights as well as having duties. In a constitutional monarchy or a democracy of the sort that exists as a rule among the present nations of Europe, the USA and, happily, a number of other states around the world, political freedom should go hand in hand with moral freedom.

Yet it must also be noted that, even after the fall of the Soviet Union and its satellites, the balance between political and moral freedom is often lost or, as in dictatorships or tyrannies, out of the question.

One problem is that moral freedom can remain purely theoretical (Kant, who defined the principles of morality in abstract terms, frequently inspires this objection). Similarly, political freedom is not always much more than a word or a slogan. In both these cases, philosophy can offer the necessary impetus to clearer thinking. The philosopher stands for freedom combined with responsibility. Therefore he has a role to play when freedom or freedoms are threatened. But he cannot make them respected on his own. The love of freedom is a good to be shared, as long as no one is exempt from its duties.

16

The question of God

Does each of us have an idea of God – that is, a being who is omnipotent, omniscient, the creator of heaven and earth? Or was the idea of God constructed over time in response to the fears and weaknesses that preyed on the human imagination, leading to belief in a superior power responsible for the origin of life and everything in it?

When Napoleon asked the celebrated mathematician and physicist Laplace, 'What becomes of God in your system of the universe?' he replied, 'Sire, I have no need of that hypothesis.' Should we conclude that Laplace got it absolutely right and that the very idea of God is as useless as it is outdated?

I am not trying to bring about an artificial reconciliation between those positive (and positivist) thinkers for whom the idea of God is obsolete and religious thinkers, who are always looking for succour (or consolation) from that quarter. Some may object that it's something you either believe in or don't. But our question is this: is it possible to argue philosophically for or against God? Not, of course, against belief or unbelief (you can't argue about them any more than you can dispute tastes) but for or against the existence of God.

Such arguments have been bandied back and forth for

hundreds of years. If the world is not wholly meaningless, it seems natural to think of it as having had an origin. Maybe its structure depends on an unbelievably intricate plan. Far from being illogical or patently absurd, the appeal to a divine creator may be just what is needed to satisfy reason's concern for universal harmony.

If this is the case, why hasn't it won over all the rationalists and, in particular, all the scientists? This objection brings us to a central point: reason's interest in universal harmony is only one form of its often excessive pursuit of coherence. The practical and natural sciences go in a different direction. Abandoning the attempt to discover one total and unified meaning, they divide reality into parts which can be determined in isolation; they describe and analyse particular functions, and derive certain rules and laws from them.

The natural sciences should not be asked to deal with the question of meaning itself, for if they did, they would lose the rigour that comes from their specificity. Nor should they try on their own to refute the alternate form of rationality which looks for the meaning of (or the key to) universal harmony.

It's true that I have referred to the positivists, philosophers who consider the very idea of God superfluous and obsolete. If the assertion of the unity of meaning is taken as a thesis, its antithesis, denying the existence of such meaning, is sure to follow. Atheism can produce rational arguments that are every bit as solid as those supporting theism. But the antithesis to theism is itself also philosophical – and not simply scientific. This is what Kant demonstrated at the end of the *Critique of*

Pure Reason. On the question of the existence of a single divine creator, there are as many arguments for as against. Reason, wanting to prove (or to disprove) the meaning of the universe, is defeated, frustrated by the oppositions that it cannot, through its own efforts, overcome.

When you find yourself at an impasse, what do you do? You retreat and change strategy. And that is indeed what Kant himself suggests. But before we listen to him on this point, it is important to emphasize that the concept of God has played a vital role in philosophy. In fact, it is possibly the keystone that holds the whole structure together.

17

So what about religion?

'I have overcome knowledge to make room for faith.' When Kant refers to his own passing from the theoretical to the practical in these words, is he trying to say that we need to give up scientific knowledge for the sake of our conversion to religion?

Kant's point, first of all, is that we can't approach practical problems in the same way as theoretical ones. In the realm of the practical, it's a question not just of knowing but of desire and will. If a rational basis for practical life is both desirable and possible, a supporting principle will have to be found. This principle is once again God, but a God whose existence cannot be proved and who cannot be represented: a moral God, a God we come to believe in as the result of a rational conviction and as an ultimate guarantor of our action.

The religion Kant preaches is one 'within the limits of reason alone'. It is a religion utterly removed from superstitious practices or even adherence to a church. It is a religion purified into the shape of a feeling, a feeling of profound respect for that 'moral law' that Kant believed is inscribed within our hearts: 'The starry heavens above us and the moral law within us.' This is the famous conclusion of the *Critique of Practical Reason*. Starting with the harmony of the senses, we must move upwards to a deeper and invisible harmony. Philosophy inherited this model from Plato and keeps returning to it.

Given the rational nature of this moral religion, it is easy to understand how Kant's disciples (especially in the second half of the nineteenth century) could end up among the ranks of the positivists, the heirs of Auguste Comte. Yet this should also be a bit surprising, because the positivist school held that the age of theology had ended. To be wholeheartedly positivist, wouldn't we need to eliminate even a moral God? Actually, positivism is very aware of a fundamental problem here. Even if religion is false, even if it rests only on myths (which are utterly fantastic narratives), it has and will continue to have an irreplaceable social role, for it enables humans to live together on good terms. What other ways are there to fulfil this function, to provide the glue for social cohesion? Despite its faults and even its dangers (the potential for fanaticism), all religion binds together, while theoretical knowledge, no matter how truthful, can offer nothing to our practical needs and desires. In the later part of his life, Comte thought he could resolve this problem by creating a new positivist religion with its own temples, rituals and so on. It was a total failure. But he did identify a problem that must be faced constantly by our advanced societies, transformed as they are by science and technology: how is it possible to find (or rediscover) a form of social cohesion that can hold society together and assure its members a harmonious life?

No doubt you will object that religions have been intolerant far too long and too often. Everyone believes they can work out the truth on their own. Yet Jesus, who preached love, said to

Pontius Pilate, 'I am the truth.' Pontius Pilate's philosophy, on the other hand, was sceptical: 'What is truth?' he asked. This may not be intoxicating, but a freethinker will remark that such scepticism is much less dangerous than the attitude that proclaims itself to be the truth. History testifies to this: the intolerance that threatens all religious thinking is manifested everywhere, in wars of religion, persecutions, the Inquisition and, today, the spread of fundamentalism.

So should philosophy be for or against religion? Philosophy can remain agnostic, but it must do its bit and contribute to the understanding of a phenomenon central to human history. It can help us to respect what is worth respecting, both in the religious attitude and in its rituals of worship, celebration, prayer and love. For faith has inspired many sacrifices and acts of devotion. And countless human beings find consolation in religious observance, especially in the face of death.

Is the conflict between philosophy and religion, then, really inescapable? Yes, if you believe that Lucretius, in the first century BC, was right to warn his contemporaries against religion: 'How much evil can be done by religion!' No, if you listen to the message of Pope John Paul II, who, in his encyclical *Faith and Reason*, said that philosophy 'is like a mirror where human culture is reflected' and is 'often the only common ground for understanding and dialogue with those who are outside our faith'.

How can we not be grateful for this recognition of philosophy's role? How can we not encourage this dialogue, since philosophy itself has been in it from the start?

18

What does happiness have to do with it?

Philosophy is a serious affair, too serious, you might say. Religion, duty, moral law – you get the point. But doesn't a balanced life also include rest and relaxation? Don't we need play to counterbalance the serious activity? And what kind of wisdom are we talking about if it leaves out happiness?

Perhaps all I need to say in reply is that you must be due a break, and you certainly deserve one, because our discussions so far have been pretty taxing.

But I prefer to take the question of happiness seriously. First posed by early Greek philosophers, it is still relevant today. At its simplest, it amounts to this: shouldn't the aim of the good and just life, the philosophical life, be the achievement of a certain happiness? Isn't this legitimate?

Right from the start we have to face the problem of how to define happiness. If you ask people in the street about their idea of happiness, their replies will undoubtedly be wide-ranging. If there is any consensus, it will probably be in those areas mentioned as 'keys' to happiness rather than in what happiness actually is. I bet that health, money, sexual or romantic satisfaction, academic or athletic success will be mentioned often. Admittedly, all these factors contribute to happiness in a big way. Yet do they constitute happiness itself? What does happiness consist of?

It would be easy to list numerous examples of depression among beautiful, intelligent, rich, young people who seem to have all they could want. What was it that they lacked? At the other extreme, there's Diogenes living naked in his barrel and proclaiming himself happy. We are familiar with his response to the Emperor Alexander, who had come to consult him: 'You're blocking my sunlight!'

Of the two men, who is happier, Diogenes the down-and-out, content with everything, or the despot, thirsty for ever more conquests, who would die on the verge of insanity in the depths of Asia?

It is undeniable that a psychological and subjective component features in happiness's complex recipe. When Aristotle considered happiness to be the soul's equilibrium, enjoyed by the virtuous man who has succeeded in living a life of study and leisure, he had a point. We may complain that this philosophical ideal is too measured and rational. But Aristotle was aware of this objection. First of all, he acknowledged the relativity and fragility of human happiness in the face of destiny, adopting as his own adage the old saying 'No one can be called happy before his last day!' And furthermore, he was very aware that most people prefer a life of immediate pleasure. Some will opt for a life of honour and achievement, but very few indeed will turn to the best life, the truly philosophical life.

If Aristotle is right, happiness has to be earned and created.

Certainly it depends partly on lucky chances. But it does not rest wholly on our good fortune in avoiding difficulties and coming through troubles without a scratch. Epicurus gave a formula for happiness that is too negative: happiness is an absence of suffering. Of course, that's not to be dismissed lightly, but isn't it an old man's dream of being secure and cocooned in his own private world?

In any case, should happiness be set up as an absolute goal? Once again, we're going to be reprimanded by Kant, ever ready to play the killjoy. For him, the aim of a rational and moral action must never be happiness. Does he forbid us from achieving it? No, but it is only acceptable if it comes as a bonus. In other words, above all and before everything else, you must want to act in accordance with duty and never in order to obtain the rewards of happiness. Either those rewards will come or they won't.

There is a residue of stoicism in this attitude: accept what happens with resignation, as long as your soul remains inwardly content. To fret and concern yourself about what does not depend on you is unreasonable. Be master of your own dwelling – that is, of your mind. The Kantian does not pursue happiness, but he does not refuse it either. Like the Stoic, he is prepared for anything, since he has done his duty.

No doubt, you will be finding all these notions, stoic as well as Kantian, much too austere. I don't deny you've got a point. But they do have the merit of making us reflect on the limitations of happiness, especially if it is conceived in a selfish manner. Is happiness really complete if it is not shared? Popular imagination, especially in France, the nation of gourmets and bon vivants, has spontaneously rediscovered the twofold tradition of Plato's *Symposium* and the Last Supper: what could be happier than a good meal eaten with friends?

I hope I have reassured you that the question of happiness is absolutely central to philosophical thought. Each one of us, before we rush headlong towards happiness, must ask ourselves about our own ideal and know how to place the bar at a reasonable level: above narrow selfishness and at a bit lower than heavenly bliss.

19

Which desires? Consciousness and the unconscious

What happens when the desire for happiness is too powerful? Then we may become very unhappy, like spoiled children frustrated because they can't get the toy they want.

What do we desire profoundly and intensely? Do we even know ourselves what we want? Is there really a truth of desire? These are questions that appear to be purely psychological but whose scope is in fact philosophical through and through.

I want what I don't have. In this sense, desire is an inclination that is not yet satisfied. But, as popular wisdom insists, it's madness to want the moon. You desire what you need. But don't we all too often want the unattainable?

When the problem remains at the level of instinctive or 'natural' desires, it may appear simple. I'm hungry, I want to eat; I eat, the desire disappears and only reappears after several hours. If all desires obeyed this logic of regular and cyclical satisfaction, we wouldn't have to go on worrying about it.

But man is a being whose desires go beyond his immediate needs, who seems to desire just for the sake of it. He is a difficult creature to satisfy because his desires are governed by a principle more demanding than that of simple physical satisfaction.

'Sublimation' is the name Freud gave to the process whereby desire is displaced on to less tangible ends, towards symbolic, intellectual or artistic objectives. Freud applied his theory of sublimation to the domain of sexuality. Sublimation would not exist if sexual desire was always and immediately satisfied at the most basic physical level. Perhaps man is a subtle and over-complicated animal, since his sexuality takes roundabout and symbolic routes. To a great extent, it is the object of an inter-nalized social control, ruled by that part of ourselves Freud calls the super-ego – the agency of censorship. Yet if we repress some part of our drives, this repression is not entirely negative, because it forces us to refine our desires.

While there is certainly some truth in this Freudian notion, it also requires us to come to a better understanding of the rela-tionship between consciousness and desire. Does consciousness always mean the thinking mind, a mind that is master of itself and its desires? Descartes celebrates the intellect as clear and distinct; for him, the principle of unshakeable certainty is located in the *cogito* ('I think'). Yet even he acknowledges that we don't always have absolute control over ourselves, since our bodies are prey to passions. While Freud believed that becom-ing aware of the mechanism of our passions allows us to regain the advantage, since reason would be in control, he taught us to have a more complex understanding of the workings of passions and the relation between consciousness and the unconscious. We should strive for clarity, certainly, without deluding our-selves that our conscious mind can always illuminate the innermost recesses of our personality. The unconscious resists that. It is, in its own way, reserved, and only reveals its deep desires indirectly – for example, through dreams (if we know how to listen to them) or certain 'unintentional acts' (like slips of the tongue).

Freud does not claim that we can (or should) ever arrive at a state of clear and untroubled awareness where we will succeed in grasping all the ruses of our unconscious. To imagine this is to yield yet again to an even subtler version of the Cartesian dream of complete mastery. Freud's primary objective as a doctor is to treat neurosis, a pathological condition that makes it difficult to cope with life. Luckily, most of us manage to find compromise solutions and achieve a more or less 'normal' existence.

Did Freud have the last word on desire and its complex relationship with consciousness? To my mind, Hegel, whom we met earlier, had a brilliant intuition whose impact has been even more decisive than Freud's. For Hegel, man is a being who always desires more than the simple satisfaction of natural needs because he desires something no inanimate object can provide: he wants recognition. Human desire is infinite; it wants to be infinitely desired. Yet how else can one be infinitely desired if not by another human being? The struggle that determines the humanity of man is the struggle for recognition, whose paradigm is the confrontation between master and slave (in which the slave struggles and works so that he will not be reduced to a thing).

What do we desire most? We now have the beginnings of an answer: to be recognized for who we are, as creatures of infinite freedom and responsibility.

Which desire?

But are we ourselves fully aware of what we are? Do we really know what other people expect of us? The struggle for recognition is never ending, because our desires are hostage to our unconscious, and we need to understand them better in order to communicate them.

20
Technology and life

In establishing psychoanalysis, Freud brought about a veritable revolution: not only did he acknowledge the role of sexuality but he also uncovered the importance of the unconscious and what he called 'the uncanny'. He never imagined that his discoveries would be reduced to a blueprint for living better. On his arrival in the USA, he is supposed to have said, 'They do not know I am bringing them the plague.' The dominant American conception of psychoanalysis as a normalizing technique pure and simple would have disgusted him.

The danger of reducing our psychological and moral life to a technical matter is twofold. On the one hand, we risk forgetting what we are living for. Can we really just act without a considered overall plan, oblivious to questions of right or wrong, good or evil, and how to decide between them? On the other hand, if it is only a matter of regulating our desires, making them function properly, as if we were getting an engine to work, then isn't our existence nothing but variations on a basic form of behaviour, explicable wholly in terms of the 'stimulus-response' mechanism?

The behaviourist would say yes. Behaviourism, a theory originating in the USA, has had considerable success and permeates every aspect of contemporary life and consumer society. We experience its effects all the time, usually without even being aware of it. For example, advertising works on a rudimentary but large-scale level in a way that is quite simply designed to manipulate our consciousness and our unconscious. What sort of people are advertisers targeting with their barrage of slogans and images? Free and responsible men and women? They are merely 'consumers', created by sampling a significant portion of the population. Television and film are even used to transmit 'subliminal messages', images slipped in so quickly that they cannot be perceived but nonetheless have an effect. All this is a long way from the subtle ruses of the Freudian unconscious, and even further from the recognition of man by man.

It is obvious that every aspect of our society has been transformed by technology. Its effects have been positive in many areas: travel, communications, everyday conveniences, our health and comfort. However, does this mean that our thoughts, our attitudes and our emotions should also be determined by technology? And isn't this exactly how we are being pushed by all the 'marketing' techniques I've mentioned? It is no longer good enough to use reasoned argument to convince or persuade people. You're being conditioned, even compelled, to accept that a certain brand of jeans or shoes is 'trendy' or 'cool'; the image of super-sleek, trim bodies is meant to remind you of low-fat yoghurt and food products. All this reduces you to a few simple behavioural reflexes. How far are these forms of manipulation going to go? Are you going to let yourself be persuaded and not react, not use your critical faculties?

'One can take it or leave it,' you reply. I gladly agree, and I hope that intelligent young people will refuse to be transformed entirely into mere consumers. However, education and culture have something to do with it. A critical mind doesn't fall from the sky; it has to be acquired, built up and perfected.

Further, if I do emphasize so strongly the negative aspects of our consumer society, it's because they reveal a more general problem that philosophy should not underestimate: whether life and existence should be viewed solely from a technological point of view. At the level of biology and medicine, how far should we go in the use and improvement of artificial reproductive techniques? Manipulation of the genetic code and, maybe in the near future, cloning? At the psychological and moral level, is it right to think of other people merely as means? For example, are parents only useful for housing and supporting me? Are my friends there to amuse me and do me favours? Does my girl- or boyfriend exist only to give me pleasure? And so on. If this is the case, then a purely mechanistic view of human life is the only one that will prevail. And then what will humanity have come to?

Technology, traditionally defined, is using means to achieve an end. But these ends must still be clearly perceived and lucidly chosen. When technologies were still simple and small scale, the relation between means and ends was easy to see. In our civilization, technology is omnipresent; it has even become a social issue. It is integrated and internalized in the way we act. Above all, it is much more than a pile of tools, equipment and machinery. Technology has never been more efficient and subtle than when it is able to converge with the sciences. Computer science is typical of the 'techno-sciences', because it involves at the same time mathematical models (software programs) and complicated electronic equipment (hardware). No one can deny that this 'techno-science' has contributed powerfully to the transformation of our lives.

Whatever their conveniences and advantages may be, can computers replace me as the judge of my actions and their motives? Computers can certainly help me and inform me. But would I on that account program my life with no other objective than efficiency? Besides, what kind of efficiency would it be? We are returning to our original questions: what is just and what is unjust, what is right and what is wrong, and how can we decide? These are not questions technology can answer.

21

Good, evil and beyond?

According to the Bible, it is as a result of sin that Adam and Eve were able to eat from the tree of knowledge; as a consequence, they were expelled from paradise. You don't have to have had a religious education to know this.

The symbolism is very powerful. The knowledge of good and evil is a double-edged sword. Things were simpler when we lived in a state of innocence; once that was lost, we had to assume the burdens of choice and responsibility.

But responsible towards whom or what? The first answer that comes to mind is towards one's own conscience. But was it really conscience that gave rise to those first prohibitions that marked the boundaries of good and evil ('Thou shalt not kill', 'Thou shalt not steal', 'Thou shalt not commit adultery')? Bergson, perhaps drawing on the memory of the forbidden fruit, formulated a simple hypothesis that is worth keeping in mind: it is primarily social prohibition that determines the boundaries of right and wrong, good and evil. The earliest moralities are self-contained – that is, ordained strictly by the rules of social behaviour. Each member of the group, tribe or clan knows exactly what he can and cannot do. The 'idea of the good' only gradually becomes independent of this restricted social origin;

only in Plato does it finally appear as the transcendent idea of good in itself, placed at the summit of the ethereal world of ideas.

If we are happy with this theory of the social origin of good and evil, isn't it tempting to extend it to the developed societies of today? Then there would be no question of an absolute good and evil, only prohibitions relative to the state of society. This kind of relativism would justify any transgression as long as social sanction and repression did not exclude it.

Yet relativism makes it impossible to establish a morality that is stable and coherent. Bergson can transcend relativism because he sees the moral sense as progressively acquiring universality and inwardness, until it reaches the status of 'open morality': one that relies less on prohibition than on incentive, on the life force or the love of others. Here social rules are not ignored, but their narrowness is overcome by a deepening of the moral sense, not by regression.

However, the knowledge of good and evil can be lost in two ways: from below and from above.

From below, is not the worst of all the will to do evil for evil's sake? We cannot ignore the fact that humanity is capable of the worst as well as the best, and that the myth of the Devil represents this extreme possibility of radical destruction.

In our time a form of evil has emerged that is perhaps more dangerous than the all-conquering vice celebrated by the Marquis de Sade: indifference. This cries out for serious analysis, as we cannot be indifferent to its consequences. To claim that everything is equally valid is untenable. But this attitude is widespread and insidious, circulating like a kind of subculture or by-product of our civilization. Encouraged by a passive and excessive consumption of television and the lack of any critical alternative, this attitude explains how the unjustifiable can so easily become commonplace, how gratuitous violence, cruelty and insensitivity become banal and systematic.

The 'response' our societies make is clearly inadequate. A campaign of repression will crush the most disadvantaged and spare the crimes of the elite. We must recognize an evolution where moral judgements, respect for others and awareness of higher values have been replaced by something else – considerations of power and domination.

Philosophy must not confuse what *is* with what *should be*. It can intervene on two levels: to assess what reality is and to develop criteria for making judgements. However responsible philosophy may be, and indeed because it is responsible, it can nonetheless never exclude the hypothesis that there may be something which can transcend good and evil.

If we turn now to art, we will get a better idea of where we are heading and what might follow as a result.

22

The elevating effects of art

What's the point of art? One can be satisfied by eating, drinking, sleeping, making love. Wouldn't some people consider that the ideal life? But, as a life, is it not pretty close to that of an animal? Without curiosity, without any interests except satisfying immediate appetites, how could that be a truly full life?

In contrast to this, genuine art can enchant us, disturb us and make us dream. Thus it takes us beyond mere instinct, but not immediately or directly. How does one become artistic, come to appreciate art, develop a strong desire for it? For music, painting, dance, with their power of fascination, can bring us joy and transform our lives, or so we believe.

Just as with philosophy, first you have to know where to start. You have to learn how to listen, to look, to have mastery of your body. Before reaching the highest aesthetic levels, before you can attempt to play the guitar, or to draw, or to leap and pirouette without being ridiculous, you need to acquire technique. But does it make sense to talk about technique here, and in what sense? Not in the technological sense, because instruments or machines are not involved. But we do use certain means because we want to achieve certain results. We begin with what our senses, capabilities, and emotions can do; we try to transform them, to improve our capabilities, until we can perform in a way that was impossible at the beginning. Thus, with the piano, you start with *do, re, mi, fa, so*; you play simple scales; then, day by day, you move on to more and more complicated exercises. Your fingers become more agile, your ear sharpens, you read the music more rapidly and so on.

In the first instance, then, art is technique. Technique and art are so close that it is often difficult to distinguish between the two. After listening to the concert of a great virtuoso, don't we say, 'What amazing technique!'? And if a bridge is solid and perfectly made, don't we call it 'a work of art'? There is a simple reason for this. Producing art isn't like breathing or eating; art is a human activity that transforms material elements, subjects them to a metamorphosis. But what is the point? But why do we do it?

Couldn't we object (the way people sometimes object to philosophy) by saying, 'What is art good for?' Certainly. We could call such an objection 'utilitarian'. It states that humanity could and should stick only to those things that are strictly useful. But where does the 'useful' begin and end? Isn't it also useful to be distracted, to play, to dream? Any theory restricting the human to the most basic needs brings us back to the first scenario: a humanity that eats, drinks, etc., with no other aim in view, with no possibility of rising any higher. Alas, we can think of experiments of this order in history, Chinese society under Mao being one example. Even the supposedly democratic, capitalist world, especially the North American world, is dominated by a vision of existence where basic or mediocre 'standards' are the rule.

Art uplifts, demands and transfigures. And that is why it disturbs. If it begins on a purely technical level, it does not remain there. How does art detach itself from technique? Kant's response was ingenious: art introduces disinterestedness and 'free play' into activities that are initially just functional. If I play the piano solely to warm up my fingers, that is not art. If I repaint my shutters, that is not art either. If I do my exercises in the morning, it isn't dance. All these activities are technical to varying degrees. It isn't simply that art is more complex: there are songs by Brassens or Trenet that are masterpieces of emotion and disarming in their simplicity, yet they uncover a dimension of play and freedom that makes us forget our everyday worries.

Does art also elevate us above the realm of morality? Can you call Bach's *Art of the Fugue* either moral or immoral? All you need to do to appreciate Vermeer's *The Lacemaker* is to open your eyes and look – there is nothing here that has either a positive or a negative moral effect. Should one use moral criteria to evaluate Béjart's ballet to Stravinsky's music for *The Rite of Spring*? Nowadays no one would dare to do that without fear of ridicule. Yet this very autonomy, essential for the freedom of the creator or the art lover, has not always been respected. The debate is still ongoing: just how far should artistic freedom extend?

When we pose this question, we rediscover another, the one we raised when talking about the possibility of transcending good and evil. It is undeniable that art lifts us out of ourselves. Whether this is the same as a moral elevation is much less certain. And when art is everything in life, when it transfigures our existence, doesn't it lead us beyond all conventional morality and even beyond good and evil?

Could the highest kind of art, life as a form of art, replace morality itself? This is a difficult question and only the boldest of all philosophers can help us to examine it.

23

Nietzsche the unclassifiable

If I did not introduce Nietzsche in my gallery of great thinkers, it was certainly not because of a lack of greatness. Rather, it's because he doesn't fit neatly into the classical Western tradition. He is a thinker who presents himself in defiance of the norm. In his last days of lucidity he would say of himself, 'I am dynamite.' His tragic fate can only enhance his exceptional reputation: in Turin, in the winter of 1888–9, when he was forty-four years old, a tearful Nietzsche threw his arms around a horse, sent out exultant postcards signed 'The Crucified' and fell into a deep depression punctuated by bouts of delirium.

Should we encourage the young to follow a philosopher as unbalanced and even 'unwise' as him? Put your minds at rest. I do not advise you to *follow* him. Besides, that would be totally contrary to the spirit of his work: he did not want to found a school in the strict sense, a school promoting a doctrine. He is writing for 'free spirits', as he announces, and Zarathustra, his 'mouthpiece', lived the life of a solitary recluse.

To tackle Nietzsche, the last thing in the world you need is to read a résumé of his 'theses'. For other philosophers – say, for Kant – there is some point to a method that starts by learning a few fundamental propositions, saving for later the task of analysing them more deeply and more systematically. With Nietzsche, this wouldn't work. His tone and style are so personal that there's no substitute for reading him.

Which is the most important book to read? For me at seventeen, it was *The Birth of Tragedy*. It is a short, passionate book, the work of a Hellenist who raised a problem often forgotten by professors of classics: how can we explain the emergence of tragedy, a unique, formally perfect art form which nonetheless contains all of life's pains and joys? It needed an extreme sensibility capable of rigorous discipline. This tension is symbolized by the battle between two antagonists: Dionysus, the god of sacred intoxication, and Apollo, the radiant god of harmony and moderation.

Compared to this tragic pair, the ironic rationality of Socrates and Plato seems like a late and decadent phenomenon. In this book Nietzsche begins a radical critique both of Socratic intellectualism and Platonic idealism.

The other text I would recommend just as highly is the prologue of *Thus Spake Zarathustra*, which announces the possible coming of the Overman. Preachers of virtue and those who despise the human body are severely reproached because they have no true understanding of either the spiritual or the physical. What man has been until now is nothing but 'a muddy stream'. He has not gone to the limit of his potential. The bow of his desires remains slack, confined to animality, content with the mediocrity always awaiting the 'last men', the modern men, those who blink their eyes and declare, 'We have invented happiness.'

Nietzsche calls into question an entire tradition that has turned its back on our earthly dwelling place to go in quest of an ideal world: the Platonic and the Christian tradition. His critique targets the ascetic morality of this tradition, a morality of renunciation, of resentment against life and against its supersensible principles (the ideal good, the God of monotheism).

So there are two complementary impulses in Nietzsche: critical and constructive. His study of morality cannot be separated from his affirmative *Yes* to life. To give form to this embracing of life, it may be that a new approach is required – that same elevation to a higher plain that is required for great art. By treating life as a form of art, do we not transcend good and evil?

We could downplay the originality of Nietzsche's ideas a bit by pointing out that Pascal had already said, 'True morality doesn't care about morality.' But for Pascal this sidestepping of morality remains within the confines of the Christian religion. It is God's grace that allows us to find the right measure beyond all human limitations, while Nietzsche means to supersede all recognized values, because 'God is dead'.

But we must not belittle the risks Nietzsche takes: he makes us leap into the unknown. Moved by the vigour of his critique of Christian morality, what would happen if we were unconditionally to accept his apologia for a 'great politics' carried on by bloody and cynical geniuses like Caesar or Napoleon?

Let's not forget that Nietzsche is not writing for the masses but for 'superior' men, who are very few in number, those 'free spirits' who constitute a veritable aristocracy of the mind. Is he right? Is he wrong? He has written unforgettable things on art because he himself is an artist as well as a thinker (and this is not the case with all the great philosophers).

What he has written on politics is much less worthy of admiration. It would be better for us here to start again from scratch, looking at humanity in its widest sense, not in order to crush it with contempt but to govern it with justice.

24

What society, which state?

Nietzsche, who is not thought of as a political philosopher, has nonetheless brought us to the question of politics. However, to draw political principles from Nietzsche's ideas would be a very risky business. The Nazis wanted to make him one of their prophets, yet they also wanted to censor him. To see him as a blend of the anarchist and the aristocrat would capture his spirit more faithfully.

Since Plato, philosophy has had to confront politics, and has tried to think through the principles and aims of political life. Philosophers have even been tempted to offer themselves as advisers to rulers, for better or for worse.

To recognize the importance of the political does not mean that 'everything is political', as some students proclaimed during the rioting in France in May 1968 (in fact, it's a totalitarian slogan, because it destroys the separation between the private and the public). What it does mean, however, is that a balanced view of man and his future cannot ignore the question of the best form the state can take, or the problem of finding a link between private morality and public status (where we find citizenship, its rights and its duties).

Common sense reminds us that ideas don't pay the bills. It

is certainly true that an exceptional political philosopher will not necessarily be an effective statesman. A philosopher reflects on his principles, he doesn't himself have to put them into practice. By the same token, an excellent treatise on medicine can be written by someone who isn't actually a medical practitioner, and vice versa. The fact that Plato failed with the tyrant of Syracuse does not diminish the interest of his *Republic*, which has nurtured political reflection for 2,500 years.

What is the situation today? We should know how to benefit from all the experience gained from the lessons of history – about the organization of society, about different constitutions, about forms of government. It is obvious that political philosophy, the beneficiary of an entire tradition of thought, has become on its own account a rich and complex area of specialization full of the sorts of precedents and references that are useful for considering the eventful development of the West. But yet again reality is not what it should be. As Hegel remarks, men hardly ever learn from the lessons of history. For all the advisers, archives full of information, computer simulations and programs that governments have at their disposal, what they most often respond to are the imperatives of the moment and the pressure of powerful interests. It is rare to come across an occasion when philosophers might have a direct influence on the course of events and political decisions.

Philosophy's greatest temptation has been, and still is, the idea of Utopia, the dream of an ideal society. Is the idea of Utopia healthy or dangerous? Its supporters assert that Utopia stimulates and refreshes the spirit: without it, politics would be reduced to the dreary realities of management. Utopia's adversaries consider it dangerous: the denial of the world's realities leads to a contempt for human beings. Robespierre, Stalin and Hitler were Utopians. Robespierre sought a virtuous and incorruptible society, while Stalin wanted an absolutely egalitarian and disciplined society, and Hitler a racially pure one. We know the results.

Political philosophy should take into account the realities of society. Aristotle does so when, in *The Politics*, he defines man as a 'political animal' and subsumes economics under politics, but most of all when he analyses the different types of constitution possible: democracy, monarchy, aristocracy (and their deviant forms). For him the best regime is not a distant ideal. It is a 'happy mean' – that is, a solution that is eminently realizable and avoids excessive harm in its resolution of the problem facing any political theory: how can men be made to live together harmoniously and under the rule of justice?

The lesson here is valid for all times and involves making a distinction between society in general (with its different types of group formation, from the family to the clan, the association, etc.) and the state, which is an institution, a legitimate and sovereign political power with a territory, a currency, an army and so on.

Not all ethical and social problems can be reduced to political problems. Nor are all political problems on a par, especially in our developed societies with their complex structures.

One of the tasks of contemporary philosophy, in this context, is to become aware of the specificities of politics in the modern sense. Many of the problems that need to be dealt with are technical (for example, establishing budgets, organizing the administration and management of personnel). Does it follow that the whole of the political sphere will become 'technical'? That a prime minister and his cabinet are nothing but managers? If politics retains a meaning, what should its role be? How will it respect moral imperatives? For the individual citizen, is there a role, a way of intervening in the state, that allows both rights and duties to be respected? All these are current and even pressing questions for a responsible political philosophy.

The ideal and the real intersect, as do rights and morality, the individual and the collective. At the point where they meet we find both reflection and political action, just as we always have. According to Bergson, any genuine man of action must be a thinking man, and vice versa. Which is to say that philosophical thought must be the flipside of political action, its critical and reflective alter ego. If not, the health of the body politic cannot be guaranteed.

25

Too many questions?

We have already tackled a good many problems from morality to politics, and from aesthetics to religion. As apprentice philosophers, are we becoming dilettantes?

I was expecting this objection, which can be put more crudely: we can't know everything! Even reduced, the syllabus is much too big!

As we are approaching the home stretch, it would be an excellent idea to pause and reflect on these objections. Taking a break like this is just the sort of thing philosophers do.

It is true that, in principle, no human problem is alien to philosophy. But no matter how intelligent and hard-working he is, no philosopher can master *all* the problems, especially in a world constantly being transformed by the rapid development of science and technology, as well as changing ways of life. That is why, at its highest levels, the study of philosophy must specialize: logic, philosophy of science, philosophy of technology, aesthetics, ethics and political philosophy are so many largely autonomous fields of study.

Does this mean that it is now impossible to practise 'pure philosophy' for its own sake? Kant thought about this difficulty (since what constituted knowledge in his day was already encyclopedic) and his response was the following: 'You cannot learn philosophy, for there is no such thing as a final philosophy, universally valid. You can only learn to philosophize.' In other words, you don't learn philosophy as if it were the sum of different branches of knowledge; the danger of becoming a philosophical encyclopedia is therefore not a real problem. One learns to do philosophy by arguing, reasoning, raising pertinent questions and examining them critically, and by acquiring intellectual maturity.

The Kantian answer is as valid for the beginner as it is for the tenured professional.

I am not claiming that you are already more than a beginner thanks to this book. But at least you are aware that each of these chapters was intended to stimulate surprise and reflection. There is no point in memorizing this book, or any other philosophy manual or treatise (it is not a discipline where all you need to do is to tick off the boxes in a questionnaire). Rather, what matters is to make a start with thinking. Of course, once you start to acquire a certain knowledge, you will familiarize yourself little by little with the vocabulary of philosophy, learn to pose a problem, to examine its different aspects, to organize a discussion and gradually approach the great writers.

Kant's lesson must not be neglected by the professional philosopher who has already accumulated a lot of knowledge. He may be knowledgeable in the field of philosophy, but has he forgotten how to philosophize? Shouldn't he learn again how to be astonished and, in each new experience of wonder, relearn how to philosophize?

Despite the fact that Bergson speaks with some justification when he claims that all true philosophy turns on simple intuition, we may not always get the same response to the question 'What is the essence of philosophy?'

Try the experiment out on the answer that comes to your mind when you hear the beginning of Hamlet's soliloquy 'To be or not to be . . .' Is this 'either–or' not the philosophical question *par excellence*? And if we could ask only one question, wouldn't it be this one?

As soon as we reflect on the question we see that it can't be understood in just one sense.

As Shakespeare conceives it, the problem is whether, by ending your life, you would know a sleep free from remorse or the prospect of Final Judgement. Expressed as the problem of 'being', the question becomes instead a decision which every free person can take in relation to his own life and the possibility of death. For Camus, this is the most important problem in philosophy. As he writes, at the beginning of his essay *The Myth of Sisyphus*, 'There is only one truly serious philosophical problem: suicide. To judge whether life is worth living or not would be to answer the fundamental question of philosophy.' Camus's response to this question, intended to be the most concrete of all possible questions, takes the form of a reflection on the human condition. Yes, the human condition is absurd; man is a being who must suffer, often for no reason; but he has the privilege of consciousness and the power to dispose freely of his life. Renouncing the struggle, choosing annihilation, is not the courageous solution. Above all, Camus directs his attack against the nihilistic conception of suicide, because it treats life with contempt and indifference. To choose the heroic solution is to assume the most noble burden: the freedom of taking life on in all its tragedy.

Can we decide if life has meaning before we have thought deeply about the very notion of meaning, the meaning of reality, about being itself? In this case, the question 'To be or not to be' is no longer an immediate existential problem but something more abstract and distant. It is no longer limited to the petty problem of my personal survival. It becomes a question of being as such, being as opposed to the void, to non-being. When I think about 'being', I can also imagine its non-existence. But when I think I am contemplating nothingness, is this 'non-being' only a derivative concept, deduced by subtracting what does exist (as Bergson thought)? Or, even if it does sound paradoxical, must we recognize nothingness as an agonizing 'reality' (as Heidegger maintained in his lecture 'What is Metaphysics?')?

In the second case, Hamlet's question takes on a much more enigmatic meaning.

Is this meaning too abstract? Perhaps. But wonder in the face of being, in the face of the very fact that there *is* being. This astonishment should be hailed and held precious, since it may be the most philosophical act of all.

26

How to approach the authors

What if this line of questioning brings out the rebel in you, or you just find yourself allergic to what has been proposed here? Let's suppose that this is the case and you prefer not to ask questions (or not too many). Without agreeing with you, I suggest that we go on with our conversation a bit longer.

Conversation, I said, not conversion. I am not out to convert you to philosophy. But I am making an appeal to your intelligence. You may perhaps respond that you have a mind for geometry but not for this sort of subtlety. That would be an interesting and informed response, because it would presuppose a distinction made by Pascal, one which credits philosophy with a certain quality: subtlety.

Note that I haven't lavished unconditional praise on philosophy and that I am not trying to present it, at all costs, as the highest possible activity. What I want particularly to demonstrate are its possibilities, its intellectual and critical resources. In case you're not yet hooked, I would like to try and discuss some further points that may enable you to overcome certain knee-jerk reactions.

For example, one day you may stumble, accidentally perhaps, on an author who suits you more than the others. One who may really do it for you. I am not going to return to the classical philosophers whom we have already met, but rather limit myself to a few practical pieces of advice on approaching those authors who may touch or excite you.

Reading a great text will give you a unique experience that no textbook, no summary, no guide and no course can provide. Suddenly you discover a style, a personal tone, a teacher, a friend. Malebranche, strolling along the banks of the Seine, opened by chance Descartes's treatise *On Man*; his life was transformed. Perhaps you too will make a similar discovery.

I sometimes wonder, letting my imagination run free, what I would have learned had I met Socrates, Plato and Aristotle in the flesh. Perhaps not a lot more than I learn from reading their texts.

Of course, you have to make the effort to read, and that demands a bit more than just listening. And even before you begin reading, you have to make a good choice. I can understand if you feel bewildered when confronted with a library of difficult works. So here are a few words of advice.

Although it is always preferable to go to the great texts, this does not mean that you must jump straight away into the *Critique of Pure Reason*, for example, reading it from beginning to end, as you would devour a fat novel. Yet if you take up the two prefaces, you may be surprised that you can understand them without too much difficulty. The same is true with Descartes: the *Discourse on Method* is a kind of preface, written in a very attractive style, including bits of narrative (about his education at the College de la Flèche, about his tastes). Wouldn't it be intriguing to attempt a little exploration?

If you are looking for a nonconformist, slightly mad original, a pitiless observer of the human heart, an invigorating pessimist, pick Schopenhauer. Rather than jumping immediately into his masterpiece, *The World as Will and Idea*, you could look for his paradoxical and surprising little book *The Art of Always Being Right*.

On the other hand, if your mind inclines more to the geometrical, and you are looking for a philosophy that will enable you to acquire the certainties to improve your scientific studies, you should turn instead to Auguste Comte, whose *Discourse on Positivism* provides the synthesis of a philosophy that aims to be rational, precise, modern and concrete. It may be, however, that his style, which manages to be methodical and rhetorical at the same time, will strike you as a bit dated. In that case, you could break into contemporary theorizing about scientific knowledge with a lively and likeable teacher, Gaston Bachelard, whose most accessible book is *The New Scientific Spirit*.

I almost forget a master of the French language, admirable for both his clarity and his educative skills: Henri Bergson. What better way to become acquainted with him than his essay on the comic? It began life as a speech for an awards ceremony, an exercise whose charms and obligations are unknown to secondary school pupils today. It is certainly not his most profound book. But his approach to the phenomenon that is the comic through examples is a model of method and patience which, in defining the subject, succeeds in retaining its tone. By the way, the book I have just been recommending to you is entitled *Laughter*.

You don't have to cry to learn philosophy.

27

Why not a science?

Before we end, it may be time to draw up a clear balance sheet on the question of the relations between philosophy and the sciences. A great many of the major philosophers have been scientists; but today in France it is the literary figures who make the running in philosophy, and philosophy is a discipline that is taught in the faculty of arts. Moreover, we have seen a large variety of positions: some philosophers like to think they are scientifically rigorous, others assume a contrary position, taking all kinds of liberties with rational or positivist methods. How are you going to find your way? To answer that, I will draw on two methods, the first historical and the second analytical.

Historically, philosophy and science arose together, in Greece, under the name of *episteme*, knowledge of what is. Science itself has never formed a homogeneous bloc. The first sages of Greece were astronomers, physicists, moralists and even doctors, all at once. It is only when we come to Plato that we see the first distinction between mathematics and philosophy as such. But distinction is not separation, and even less is it opposition. At the entrance to his Academy Plato had these words written: 'Let no one ignorant of geometry enter here.' For him, geometry is a first absolutely essential stage in the ascent to the world of ideas. The Platonic tradition is so positively inclined towards mathematics that Galileo could find support in Plato (against the Aristotelians) when he founded mathematical physics in the modern sense. But Aristotle himself, although less of a geometer than Plato, was a great logician, and a biologist without equal. In his day, he was a tremendous scientist. And if we line up the great modern philosophers, starting with Bacon (pioneer of the experimental method), Descartes (inventor of analytic geometry, expert in mechanics, optics, cosmology), Leibniz (inventor of the infinitesimal calculus), we see that the divorce between science and philosophy is relatively recent.

So is it even necessary to speak of a divorce? Let's focus our minds on the present delimitations in the fields of science and philosophy.

In principle, every science has a determinate object: mathematics studies numbers and quantitative relationships; physics material nature; biology living things. In fact, in our time each of these sciences has divided the scope of its work into increasingly narrow subdivisions. In physics, for example, theoretical physics is distinguished from the physics of elementary particles, but also from condensed-matter physics, from astrophysics, and so on.

Can philosophy be a science like all the others? If philosophy lacks a specific object, reflecting instead on the conditions in which the other sciences are possible, the reply must be in the negative. Yet this reply, in its turn, can be understood in a negative and a positive sense.

Negatively, the conclusion would be that philosophy cannot be a rigorous form of knowledge like the other sciences.

Accordingly, it must be either rejected or made strictly subordinate to the sciences. Such an attitude is what we call scientistic.

Positively, only philosophy examines the fundamental questions that the sciences themselves cannot raise without transgressing the very limits that define them. If a biologist wonders 'What is life?' he is no longer being a biologist. In actual fact, scientists frequently ask themselves philosophical questions regarding their own discipline. The most lucid of them do so deliberately and with self-awareness – that is, without intending to preach either to their scientific colleagues or to philosophers. They are extremely conscious of the difficulty of the enterprise. Einstein managed to formulate his own philosophical propositions, such as, 'God does not play dice' or 'The most incomprehensible thing about reality is that it is comprehensible.' He never confused these reflections with his scientific work.

It is because it's in the nature of philosophical thinking to be both general and fundamental that philosophy was long given the privilege of being considered 'the queen of sciences'. No one would support such a view now. There is no longer a sovereign science; there is not even a single paradigm for what a scientific approach should be.

There are those who are tempted to invert the priorities here, looking down on any concern that is not scientific. Yet isn't such 'hard' scientism an overreaction, more passionate and less rational than it pretends to be, trapped in an overly schematic conception of science and misunderstanding the possibilities of rigour and analysis that belong to the work of philosophy? Those philosophers who adopt a scientistic position, if they resort to argument, remain philosophers (this is the case with Carnap and the neopositivists of the Vienna School). Their main concern is to show that philosophy can assert itself as a rigorous discipline as long as it renounces its earlier claims. Although this concern is in principle perfectly respectable, its concrete consequences warrant further discussion. Everything depends on the extent of the 'remainder', the domain designated as the preserve of philosophy.

Following on from this, we have the right to pose a few more questions to the scientistic thinkers. Is your conception of rigour overly restrictive? Is there only one way to arrive at truth? Is there only one kind of truth?

28

Justice and truth

Do the sciences have an answer for everything? In one essential sphere they need to be taken over and guided and that sphere is ethics. There is no science that can tell us if the exploitation of atomic energy, the exploration of space or the possible cloning of human beings is morally good or bad. And even if it has to take into account more and more scientific information, ethics is not itself a science. Its interest in ends puts it at the very heart of philosophy.

The aim of ethics assigned by Aristotle was 'to live a good life'. Not much to disagree with there. But determining what constitutes 'good' is not straightforward: between the useful, whose limitations we have come to know, and the good in itself – radiant, like a dazzling star – there is the just. But isn't this, in turn, simply a timid compromise to avoid violence and conflict? Or is it rather the lucid, if complex, elaboration of all the best solutions we can find and the best decisions we can take to ensure social harmony and individual happiness? If the latter, we must construct *A Theory of Justice* (the title of a work by the American philosopher John Rawls), even if justice should never remain purely theoretical.

This is the wide-ranging syllabus that makes up the

practical side of philosophy. How can we work through it without a concern for truth? Theory and practice are closely linked: a theory that doesn't lead to actual practice remains abstract and provisional; a practice lacking clarification by theory is comparable to a car driving at night without headlights.

To declare that philosophy's theoretical side is the search for truth seems obvious. If there is a difficulty, it lies in the singular designation: does it refer to truth in general or to 'The Truth' (assuming that there is a higher and unique truth)? Neither of these alternatives is completely satisfactory.

When Pontius Pilate and Jesus had their extraordinary confrontation, the Roman procurator posed the philosophical question *par excellence*: 'What is truth?' However, he seems to have done so in a tone of profound scepticism. Even admitting for a moment that Pilate was right to believe that there is no proper answer to such a question, is it not in fact philosophy's task to show how this search for truth is an infinite and impossible quest? If the other response offered, that of Jesus (who presents himself as 'the way, the truth and the life'), demands faith, then it is not philosophical.

The philosophical search for the truth cannot claim to be exclusive without contradicting itself. For truth is not written in capital letters. Philosophy's unique privilege is not that it can present its own truths (even supposing it could establish any) as superior to religious or scientific truths. Rather, it is privileged because it reflects on the very notion of truth and on the conditions that govern valid judgement. Hence philosophical thinking must be specific and narrowly conceived, not like the search for a general truth. Philosophical thought appears only at the end of a cultural evolution that has already enabled humanity to discover many different truths at many different levels.

Is it necessary to reject everything that claims to be true? Aristotle's answer would be, 'No one is left completely outside the gate.' He means that truth is not unified and is not given as a whole, but reveals itself bit by bit through experience and trial. Philosophy's role is not to condemn errors but to correct and overcome them, confirming as true only those claims whose truth and validity can be tested. Which must lead us to pose questions such as the following: 'Is truth a function of the form of the judgement itself, or is it a matter of a correspondence with external reality?' 'Is a true judgement irrefutable?' 'Are there truths that cannot be demonstrated?' 'Is logical truth the only kind of truth?' and so on.

Truth and justice, justice and truth: they are the two sides of an appropriate banner for philosophy. Yet what is a banner but a sign of pride, a sign of identity. It's what a noble fighter might use to rally members of his clan, his family or his nation.

One could well imagine the philosophers thus grouping themselves on a battlefield. But isn't philosophy primarily the love of wisdom and doesn't it speak to everyone? Thus it must not transform its objectives into slogans.

29

Which kind of love?

Plato's finest dialogue, *The Symposium*, is devoted to love, to the god of love, Eros, and to different forms of love. In the course of a convivial dinner party, each of the guests makes an effort to speak in praise of love.

We, the inheritors of a long Judaeo-Christian tradition, might expect to see carnal, physical love treated as soiled, guilty, something to be despised. Nothing of the sort. But the most astonishing thing is that love in this dialogue takes on a philosophical value, even becoming the representative of our ascent towards the world of ideas, although Plato does not conceal the fact that love is also responsible for delirium and distraction because it first desires beautiful bodies made of flesh and blood, and so falls far short of ideal purity.

The expression 'platonic love' is misleading. It implies that Plato completely outlawed physical love, and this is not the case at all. What is true, on the other hand, is that he believed that physical love needs to be illuminated by the higher harmony of which it is a reflection. Further, it represents one phase of our ascent towards the beautiful and the good.

Undeniably, this conception of love is very intellectual, perhaps too much so. Even in the Bible you can find, in the

Song of Songs, more sensual and carnal evocations of love. Yet the Platonic ideal doesn't lack nobility. It reveals how much philosophy, if it remains in touch with life itself, moves us the way desire moves us, leading us to transcend ourselves and inspiring us with enthusiasm, drawing us towards the divine.

After Plato, is philosophy without love possible? Isn't love even embedded in the very word 'philosophy'? Yet is it a love young people today would want or could share? There are, of course, contemporary forms of it: for example, you could read *Death in Venice* by Thomas Mann (which inspired the film by Visconti). It is a meditation, set in the most beautiful of cities, on the impossible love of an elderly professor, Aschenbach, for the ideal form of a young adolescent, Tadzio.

Would you consider this meditation too philosophical and too removed from real life? Who is ready to find the reflection of ideal beauty and the good in their girlfriend or boyfriend? 'That's too high-flown for us!' you will insist.

It is exactly this difference that Plato wanted to emphasize. He never sought to rally to his side the majority of ordinary people. His is an aristocratic notion of love (*aristos* means the best). Yet isn't a philosophy that is modern and democratic supposed to agree with Christianity in advocating universal love?

By declaring, 'Love one another,' Jesus has left us an unforgettable command that, alas, is invariably ignored. Why? Yet again, philosophy must take into account reality: the love of one's neighbour is probably too abstract to be genuinely shared. In Nietzsche's view, there was only one Christian and he died on the cross. The evangelical ideal, like all philanthropy, is an inaccessible and impractical Utopia that conceals a spirit of revenge against the selective character of life.

Nietzsche recommended something he called 'love at a distance', a love that elevates and forms hierarchies; the heights it aspires to represent life's hidden possibilities. Even though he claimed to reverse Platonism, Nietzsche rediscovered the route of higher philosophical love and saw that it was the way to rise above ordinary humanity.

What this debate shows is the extent to which the question of love remains central to philosophy today. The respective roles of physical desire and attachment to a person continue to provoke discussion throughout the philosophical tradition. While sexuality was repressed for many hundreds of years, today its vindication intrudes in every aspect of life – all too often in forms that are violent or artificially manipulated by advertisements and the media. We have passed from one extreme to the other.

Do we know the right tasks for a philosophical way of thinking that is conscious of recent developments and has been enlightened by the discoveries of psychoanalysis and the human sciences? We do know that it should not reduce human love to its most basic expression. It should consider human love in all its different forms with tolerance and sympathy and it should give love the chance to contribute again to the search for wisdom.

30

A few seeds of wisdom

Wisdom is the practical aim of philosophy. But it is outdated. Almost invariably the sage is presented as a venerable old man, impressive or genial, very rarely with the features of a young girl or young man. Our age prefers extremes. Moderation repels.

Solomon had already judged that wisdom is impossible without the help of God. The monotheistic religions distrust any heightened state of the soul that might be attained independently of divine grace. Clearly, wisdom has very few friends.

Even philosophy is not so sure about wisdom. Socrates, whom the oracle at Delphi designated the wisest of men, refused the title and inaugurated this (false?) philosophic modesty that involves saying one is only a lover or friend of wisdom, differentiating himself from those early Greek philosophers who did not hesitate to call themselves (or to have themselves called) *sophoi* – sages.

Wisdom, even if it is taken into consideration, is something *sought after* rather than possessed. But why is it considered so difficult, if not impossible, for human beings to achieve? We can understand why the religions dependent on the Bible maintain this impossibility, because for them it is the result of Adam's sin. But why philosophy?

It is philosophy's lucidity about the human condition, feeble and controlled by passion, that leads it to scepticism and can even drive it to disenchantment. Think of Voltaire's ironic modesty in *Candide* ('Cultivate your garden!') or the paradoxes of Erasmus in *In Praise of Folly* ('Know how to use your folly wisely!').

Descartes had a more measured and confident position: lacking the sovereign, omniscient wisdom that is the privilege of God, man can endeavour to master his passions, learn how to know them, and, if he knows how to limit his desires, attain a state of bliss adapted to his own limits (just as a small vessel is easier to fill than a large one).

This is how modesty can point the way on the path to wisdom. It seems to be true that the exercise of philosophy, teaching us to be clear about the world and about ourselves, can teach us moderation and measure and thus also be the beginning of wisdom.

If the greatest philosophers hesitated to call themselves sages, what can be said about us modest apprentices? What counts, in truth, is not the label or the rank one is given: it is the path actually taken.

While our technological society emphasizes adaptation and flexibility, our decision-makers fuss about integration, responsibility, the sense of citizenship. The question of individual balance, the sense of what counts in life, seems to be downgraded to a mere accessory. And those who refuse the dominant model are considered dropouts: our society wants to be efficient, controlling and profitable.

Despite everything, I was determined to conclude with

wisdom, because I do not think it is anachronistic, provided that one knows how to love it and find in it a new face, a fresh palette. This does not inevitably mean a trip to India. But it means something like a serious examination of what really should count in life, something a bit like a pilgrimage to the source after all.

It's up to you to take it from here. A living practice of philosophy always includes a personal side in addition. Over and above the academic success that you can legitimately seek, life is waiting for you with its pitfalls and its joys. Why not go out to meet it with a bit of philosophy?

If you think I may be right, you will sow these few seeds of wisdom and they will blossom as if they were in your own secret garden.

Further reading

Classic texts

René Descartes, *Discourse on Method and Meditations on First Philosophy*, trans. D. Cress, 4th edn, Hackett Pub. Co., 1999

Georg Hegel, *Introduction to the Philosophy of History*, trans. L. Rauch, Hackett Pub. Co., 1997

Immanuel Kant, first and second prefaces to the *Critique of Pure Reason*, trans. N. Kemp Smith, Palgrave Macmillan, 1995

Friedrich Nietzsche, *On the Genealogy of Morality and Other Writings*, eds K. Ansell Pearson & C. Diethe, 1994

Blaise Pascal, *Pensees*, trans. A. J. Krailsheimer, Penguin, 1995

Plato, *The Symposium*, trans. C. Gill, Penguin, 2003

Contemporary introductions

Julia Annas, *Ancient Philosophy: A Very Short Introduction*, Oxford University Press, 2000

Keith Ansell Pearson, *How to Read Nieztsche*, Granta, 2005

Julian Baggini and Jeremy Stangroom, *New British Philosophy: The Interviews*, Routledge, 2002

Simon Blackburn, *Think: A Compelling Introduction to Philosophy*, Oxford University Press, 2001

Edward Craig, *Philosophy: A Very Short Introduction*, Oxford University Press, 2002

Further reading

Simon Critchley, *Continental Philosophy: A Very Short Introduction*, Oxford University Press, 2001

Gary Gutting, *French Philosophy in the Twentieth Century*, Cambridge University Press, 2001

Ray Monk, *How to Read Wittgenstein*, Granta, 2005

Index

Index

Index

Index

Index

Index

philosophical modern stars 29–32
philosophical schools 29
philosophical stars of antiquity
    25–8
philosophy
    as an activity vii
    for and against philosophy as a
        science 93–4
    as agnostic 56
    analytical 35
    assessing what reality is 71
    the basic question of vii
    with a capital 'P' vi, 13–14
    derivation of the word vii, 11–12
    developing criteria for making
        judgements 71
    the practical aim of 102
    role regarding truth 98
    with a small 'p' vi, 14
    specializing 84
    vague use of the word 10–11
    vital role of concept of God 53
philosophy of science 84
philosophy of technology 84
physics 93
Pilate, Pontius 56, 97
Plato 13, 14, 25, 55, 80, 89
    and geometry 92–3
    Hippias Major 21, 24
    his vision ix
    and ideas 21, 22, 23, 70
    and love 99, 100
    Parmenides 26
    personality 27
    prefers rule by an elite 48–9
    rationality 77
    The Republic 26, 81
    The Sophist 26
    The Symposium 60, 99
    use of dialogue vi, 26–7
    wonder 36

'platonic love' 99
Platonic tradition 78, 93
Platonism 26–7, 101
police states 7
political freedom
    and antiquity 48–9
    and moral freedom 49–50
    painstakingly defined and
        circumscribed 49
    a very late acquisition 49
political life 41
political philosophy 80–3, 84
politics
    and the idea of Utopia 81–2
    Nietzsche and 79, 80
    technical problems 82–3
positive thinkers 51
positivism 38, 51, 52, 55
prehistory 41–2, 43
priestly caste (Egypt) 48
'primitive people' 42
'progress' 43
psychoanalysis 65, 101
public status 80
Pyramids 13

questionability of things vii
questions, pertinent, 37

rationality 77
Rawls, John: *A Theory of Justice* 96
reality 22, 52, 71, 81, 87, 94, 100
reason 32, 52, 53, 54, 62
received ideas 5
recognition 63–4
reflection 2, 3, 34
reflex 45
relativism 70
religion
    charismatic 39
    and intolerance 55, 56

Index

Index